Making Progress in Primary Science

This book is for teachers and student teachers looking to improve their practice in primary science. Throughout the book, the focus is on the learning of science as an investigative process through which pupils develop an understanding of ideas. This is supported by modules on different aspects of teaching and learning in science, including:

- Building on children's own ideas
- How to ask and answer questions
- Managing practical work in the classroom
- Science for very young children
- Effective assessment, self-assessment and feedback
- Cross-curricular links
- ICT and science
- Science outside the classroom

Each module comprises of an introduction to the aspect; workshop materials to help you reflect on teaching, planning and managing primary science; and suggestions for further reading.

This is a companion to the book for course leaders using *Making Progress in Primary Science, 2nd edition*. It follows exactly the same module structure and can be used by participants during their course and as a useful resource afterwards. It is also designed to be used by teachers and student teachers independently of a set course.

Wynne Harlen OBE is Visiting Professor at the Graduate School of Education, University of Bristol. **Chris Macro** was a Senior Lecturer in Primary Science at Edge Hill College of Higher Education and is now a part-time lecturer. **Kathleen Reed** is Education Adviser in the Learning and Development Directorate of Milton Keynes Council. **Mike Schilling** was Deputy Director of the Centre for Research in Primary Science and Technology at Liverpool University, and now works as a consultant.

Making Progress in Primary Science

A study book for teachers and student teachers

Wynne Harlen, Chris Macro, Kathleen Reed and Mike Schilling

RoutledgeFalmer
Taylor & Francis Group

LONDON AND NEW YORK

First published 2003
by RoutledgeFalmer
11 New Fetter Lane, London EC4P 4EE

Simultaneously published in the USA and Canada
by RoutledgeFalmer
29 West 35th Street, New York, NY 10001

RoutledgeFalmer is an imprint of the Taylor & Francis Group

© 2003 Wynne Harlen, Chris Macro, Kathleen Reed and Mike Schilling

Typeset in Palatino and Frutiger
by Keystroke, Jacaranda Lodge, Wolverhampton
Printed and bound in Great Britain
by TJ International Ltd, Padstow, Cornwall

British Library Cataloguing in Publication Data
A catalogue record for this book is available from the British Library

Library of Congress Cataloging in Publication Data
   Making progress in primary science : a study book for teachers and
student teachers / Wynne Harlen . . . [et al.].
      p. cm.
Includes bibliographical references and index.
1. Science—Study and teaching (Elementary) 2. Inquiry (Theory of
knowledge) I. Harlen, Wynne.

LB1585 .M28 2003
372.3′5—dc21   2002033310

ISBN 0–415–28441–4

Contents

MODULE 1   Learning science through enquiry – starting from children's ideas   3

In this module direct experience of practical enquiry is used as a basis for reflection on what it involves. The nature of learning through enquiry, the role of children's initial ideas and of process skills in developing understanding are considered. The implications of taking children's own ideas into account when teaching science are discussed and there are opportunities to identify ways of accessing these ideas.

MODULE 2   The teacher's role in promoting progress   16

This module involves practical activity which is used to define enquiry skills and to enable participants to recognise them in practice. Approaches to developing both skills and ideas are considered.

MODULE 3   Teachers' questions and responses to children's questions   27

In this module we identify the type and wording of questions which encourage children to express their ideas and to develop their enquiry skills. We discuss how to categorise and respond to children's questions and how to handle the 'difficult' ones that children ask.

involving children in self-assessment. Peer assessment is also considered.

This module considers the science learning which might take place
out of school. There is the opportunity to consider the local guidance in respect of school visits with particular reference to the legal
aspects and the safety issues. Participants consider how the local
environment, both natural and man-made, can provide a focus for
scientific enquiry and examine research in order to think about how
interactive science centres might be used.

This module considers the different ways in which science subject
leaders can evaluate planning and practice within their schools.
Work sampling and classroom observations are discussed and consideration is given to the methods of providing effective feedback.
The role of governors and senior management teams is evaluated.

Acknowledgements

Thank you to the children and teachers at Thatto Heath Community Primary School, St Helens, Merseyside, and Legh Vale Community Primary School, Haydock, St Helens, Merseyside.

Thank you also to Joanne Edwards and Janet Skelton: PGCE trainees at Edge Hill College of Higher Education.

Figure 15.4 by S. Schwartzenberg © Exploratorium, www.exploratorium.edu

We would also like to thank Liverpool University Press for the use of illustrations from SPACE publications and Heinemann Education for the use of extracts from *Primary Science: Taking the Plunge*, 2nd edition.

Introduction to the Study Book

This book is a companion to the workshop materials entitled *Making Progress in Primary Science, 2nd edition*, a set of sixteen modules designed for use in initial training and professional development workshops, each dealing with a general aspect of teaching science in the primary school. These modules both advocate and exemplify active learning through engagement with ideas, materials and emerging educational issues. The workshop material contains activities for teachers which are intended for discussion in groups so that activity can be accompanied by reflection and analysis with others. This book has been written to enable those who study alone to share in the reflection and analysis by including all the activities and providing discussion of them and feedback that gives access to others' ideas. It will also be helpful to those who attend a course and wish to revisit material covered or to go beyond it to study other modules not included on the course.

The aim of the material is that, through active learning, the reader becomes familiar with the meaning of learning science through enquiry and with the teacher's and pupils' roles in developing scientific understanding in this way. In active enquiry learning, learners bring their experience and initial ideas to bear in trying to answer questions or understand new events and phenomena. It is the same for adults and for pupils in school. In science, this means making sense of new experience and building understanding of scientific ideas through practical investigation, through sharing and exchanging ideas with others and through consulting reference sources including experts, books, the Internet and databases. By working in this way with this material, on tasks at their own level, teachers and trainees develop the skills and knowledge to work in the same way with children.

HOW THIS BOOK WORKS

It is important for the reader to work through the activities, answer the questions and reflect on the experience before reading the related sections of discussion. Each module begins with an introduction which provides an overview of the activities and their purpose, then provides the activities, includes a discussion and reflection section, and ends with suggestions for further reading. The modules cover enduring issues relating to practical work, planning, handling questions, the teacher's role in providing for progression and continuity in development of enquiry skills and conceptual understanding. They also pay particular attention to recent developments relating to assessment, the use of ICT, science in the early years, using out-of-school resources and in-school evaluation of provision for science. The modules can be used in any sequence, although there is an obvious starting point in Module 1 for those unfamiliar with learning through enquiry and the two modules dealing with ICT fit together. There is also a series of five modules relating to assessment with an obvious sequence to them.

Wynne Harlen
Chris Macro
Kath Reed
Mike Schilling

Module 1 Learning science through enquiry

Starting from children's ideas

INTRODUCTION

This module is about learning through enquiry. This is just a way of describing learning in which process skills (or enquiry skills) are used to gather evidence to test whether certain ideas can explain phenomena and events in the world around us. Learning this way is important for several reasons. First, we are concerned to develop *understanding*, and understanding depends on the learners working things out for themselves. This is as true for adults as for children; we understand something when we have made sense of it in our own way and it fits with our experience and ways of thinking about related events or phenomena. So personal involvement in sense-making is important. When we are given isolated facts without being able to relate them to our own way of looking at things, we can only 'learn' them by rote memorisation. While there is place for memorisation (in learning the names given to things, for example), this does not help us understand and develop concepts that enable us to make sense of new experience and apply it in decisions in our daily lives.

A second reason for its importance is that learning through enquiry reflects the way that scientific knowledge is advanced through the activity of scientists. In arriving at explanations of phenomena, scientists normally use existing ideas, make predictions based on them and then make observations to see whether the predictions fit the facts. Sometimes the ideas linked are not the most obvious and that is where creativity comes into science, but once an idea is linked, then the prediction, testing and interpretation are carried out rigorously. A third reason is that enquiry is in tune with the way children learn. At the primary level, thinking and doing are closely related and understanding depends on children being able to see and work things out for themselves.

So while enquiry learning is not the only kind of learning, it is a most important one for primary science. We cannot put ready-made ideas into children's heads. They have to be built up gradually, at each point making sense of the experience that the children have. This means that ideas will always be changing, as experience grows and challenges earlier ideas. Indeed, this is true of science, too. Steven Hawking reminds us of this:

> Any physical theory is always provisional, in the sense that it is only a hypothesis: you can never prove it. No matter how many times the results of experiments agree with some theory, you can never be sure that the next time the result will not contradict the theory. On the other hand, you can disprove a theory by finding even a single observation that disagrees with predictions of the theory.
>
> (Hawking, 1988, p. 10)

So we should expect there to be change in children's ideas as they learn. A good deal of this change will be in making 'small' ideas into 'bigger' ones. Big ideas are ones that are applicable to, and link together, a range of phenomena, while 'small' ideas relate to specific situations or things but have limited application beyond them. We have to start with the small ideas and build them into bigger ones. The process cannot be done the other way round.

It is consistent with these points that in order to study enquiry learning, we should have first-hand experience of it. So the first activity in this module asks you to undertake an enquiry. Activity 1 presents a situation in which a question is posed about shadows made in coloured light. You are asked to make a prediction about what happens before trying it in practice. It is really important for you to think about the situation that is described and make your predictions before you carry out the activity. It will help you to think these things through if you write down your predictions and your reasons and your answer to part (iii). If you do not have access to laboratory equipment, you can use coloured domestic light bulbs (Christmas lights might serve) or torches covered with coloured cellophane. Do this in a room that is as dark as possible or put a curtain round a table with the equipment set up underneath.

After you have seen what happens, then comes the reflection on what you have done and thought. You are asked to stand back and think about what you did and how it affected your ideas, in this case, about coloured light. To assist in this reflection, a framework for thinking about enquiry is introduced. This is intended to help in identifying the process, or enquiry, skills and to show how they interact with and influence ideas, a key feature of enquiry.

After using the framework to analyse your own enquiry, in Activity 2 you use it to analyse the activity of children, presented in two vignettes. These high-light a second key feature of learning through enquiry, the role of the ideas that the children already have formed about the situation they are investigating. It is now well established by research and teachers' experience, that children do form ideas about the scientific aspects of the world around them long before we intervene to 'teach' them. These ideas have been formed by the children through thinking about everyday experiences, but because these experiences are limited, and sometimes their thinking processes are immature, their views often differ from the scientific view. Activity 3 presents a few examples of children's ideas that have been found to be quite widely held. As you consider them in detail you are asked to think about the implications for trying to help the children develop more scientific concepts. This serves to bring to light the importance of finding out children's ideas and Activity 4 concerns identifying ways of doing this for children of different ages.

Activity 1

(a) Start by thinking about this problem.

In a darkened room there is a white screen with an opaque ball held between it and two light bulbs, one green and one red. Each light casts a shadow on the screen and there is a place where the shadows overlap.

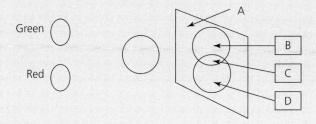

Figure 1.1 Properties of light

Answer these questions:

(i) What will be the colours on the screen in the areas, A, B, C and D?
(ii) What are your reasons for these answers?
(iii) If the white screen is replaced by a matt black one, what difference would that make? Why?

(b) Now try it in practice.
(c) Decide whether your findings have confirmed your ideas or made you rethink your ideas about light.

Activity 2

Choose either the account of Emma and the seeds, or Gavin and the Coke can, given in the box below. Analyse the activities in terms of the process skills in the enquiry model. Use the blank enquiry framework in Figure 1.2 to record your answers.

Activity 2 *continued*

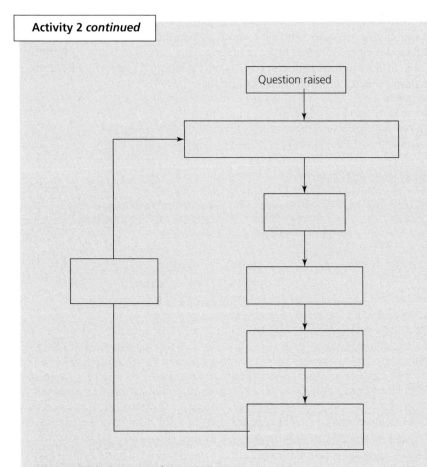

Figure 1.2 Blank enquiry framework

Emma and the seeds

The 6 and 7 year olds were collecting different kinds of seeds with a view to planting some of them in the classroom or the school garden. They included some mung bean seeds, broad bean and pea seeds, lupin and nasturtium and acorns. After the children had examined them, and added a few more from home, the teacher discussed with them whether they thought they would grow. Several children thought that the peas and beans would not grow, because 'we eat these; they are food'. She then asked them what they thought the other seeds would need to make them grow. All the children thought they needed soil and a few mentioned water. The teacher showed them some dry soil and asked them if they thought the seeds would grow in this. They then all agreed that the seeds need water. Emma was sure that they needed both soil and water – for food and drink. That was why people put them in the ground!

The teacher summarised this discussion: 'So we think that the seeds will grow if they have water and soil. What do you think will happen if they have only soil or only water?' Emma was sure they would not grow. So in a 'let's see' step the teacher guided them to think of what they could do to see if they were right. They decided to try some seeds with water only, some with soil only and some with both. The water-only ones were put on damp cotton wool. Each group of children tried all the seeds in the three different ways. They looked at their seeds daily and by the end of a week the mung beans were sprouting in the damp soil and on the damp cotton wool. In a few weeks the peas began to sprout also. The teacher discussed with Emma's group what they thought about the seeds growing without soil. At first Emma said that they were getting their food from the cotton wool. So they tried some other seeds without any cotton wool, just water. But before there was time for these seeds to sprout, the mung beans were growing up and the seed covers were pushed up with the leaves. Emma said that the seeds were 'empty' and the plant grew inside. The teacher suggested that the seed had the food for it to start growing and so all they needed was water. She asked Emma and her group to think about whether the food we eat as peas and beans is the food that the peas and beans have ready for them to grow.

Gavin and the Coke can

Like many children, 11-year-old Gavin tried to explain the wetness on the outside of a can of Coke just after it had been taken from the fridge in terms of water leaking through the metal from inside. He knew it was not Coke that was on the outside, because it was colourless and tasted like water, but he was quite prepared to explain this by saying that the metal only allowed the water in the drink to pass through. In order to work towards a more scientific explanation the teacher asked Gavin and his group to predict what would happen if an empty Coke can was cooled and then taken out of the fridge. They tried this and at first the observation of wetness forming was explained in terms of the can being still wet inside. So they were asked to find a way of getting a can quite dry inside. This they did by taking the top off, drying it thoroughly and filling it with dry cotton wool. She also asked them to think about the conditions in which the moisture formed and where else they had noticed surfaces misting over. So when they found the mist still forming on the can without water in it, they were already thinking about other reasons. One of them mentioned the bathroom mirror misting when they were too long in a hot shower and they thought it might be something to do with warm moist air meeting a colder surface. They planned further investigations to test out this idea.

Activity 3

Here are some examples of how children explain various phenomena that they observe:

(a)   Asked whether a tree is a plant, a 10 year old replied that it isn't now that it is a tree, but it was a plant when it was little (Osborne and Freyberg, 1985, p. 7).

(b)   An 8 year old explained the rust appearing on a nail: 'There is a liquid in the nail which leaks out of the nail. This forms big bumps as it leaks out. This liquid only comes out when it is wet. There must be some sort of signal to tell it to leak' (ASE, 1998).

(c)   A 10 year old drew the picture in Figure 1.3 of what he thought was inside a hen's egg when it was incubating.

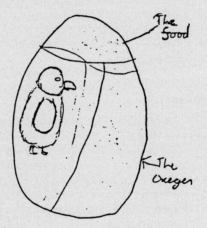

Figure 1.3 Child's idea of incubation

Source: SPACE Research Report (1992, p. 31)

(d)   An 8 year old drew the picture in Figure 1.4 of what is inside her body.

(e)   When asked about why we can't see in the dark, a 9 year old explained: 'With no light your eyes cannot see anything. As soon as you turn the light on your eyes can see again. Your eyes sort of work like a light, when there's not light you can't see but when there is light you can see again' (quoted in Harlen, 2000, p. 51).

Activity 3 continued

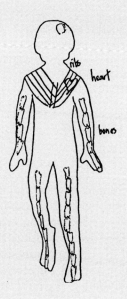

Figure 1.4 Child's idea of the human body

Source: SPACE Research Report (1992, p. 33)

For each one discuss how the children might have arrived at these ideas as a result of early experiences, or applying ideas from other sources.

What are the implications for helping children to change their ideas to the more scientific view? Fill in the grid in Figure 1.5.

	How the ideas might have been formed	Implications for developing scientific understanding
(a)		
(b)		
(c)		
(d)		
(e)		

Figure 1.5 Pro-forma: implications for developing scientific understanding

Activity 4

How can a teacher find out the ideas that children have already formed so that they can be taken into account in science activities? List as many different ways as possible and give your views on the age group for which each one is suitable.

DISCUSSION AND REFLECTION

Activity 1

If you found something different from what you predicted, you may like some help in thinking about coloured lights. The colour of a surface is the colour of light that it reflects (into your eye so that you can see it). In white light (composed of all the colours of the spectrum) a surface that looks red is reflecting just the red light and absorbs all the other colours, because of the pigment in the surface. When red light falls on a white surface (which reflects all the colours), it looks red because it can only reflect the light that is falling on it. If both red and green light fall on a white surface, both are reflected and together they make yellow. (When mixing light, red, green and blue are the primary colours and all other colours can be made by mixing them.) A surface that is really black reflects no light at all. So the black will look black whatever the colour of light falling on it. (If your black surface was a little shiny, then it may have reflected some light.)

Although you may, or may not, have learned something about coloured light from this, the main value of doing it is to be able to reflect on the process of enquiry. Think about what you were doing from the point at which you were given the situation and the questions to think about. Now consider the framework in Figure 1.6 for describing enquiry.

Can you relate your actions to the components of this framework? In this case the initial question was raised for you, but it was your own ideas about light that were used in making the predictions. Although the reasons were given after the predictions, the ideas behind the reasons were the ones used in making the predictions. If at the interpretation stage you found that your predictions were not confirmed by the evidence, it was the ideas that had to change. If your predictions were confirmed, then the initial idea was strengthened by successful application in this situation. The feedback loop to the idea passes through the 'communication and reflection' box. Communication, by talking about what was found, or writing about it, helps a learner to go over the enquiry in their mind and reflect on what the evidence means in relation to the initial ideas. In the school context it is important for children to talk about what they found and how it makes them rethink their initial ideas. Unfortunately it is often the case that an activity is thought to be finished when results are obtained and the thinking about the meaning of the results in terms of understanding is neglected.

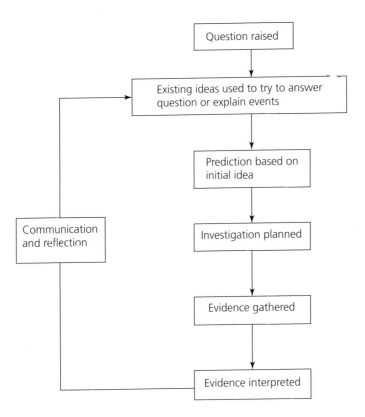

Figure 1.6 Enquiry framework

The model also indicates the inter-relationship between ideas and enquiry skills. If the skills are not carried out in a rigorous manner, for example, if the observations are not carefully made, or, in the case of 'fair testing' the variables are not controlled, then it may well be that ideas that should be changed are erroneously confirmed. This, indeed, is how children hold on to their non-scientific ideas, for they do not test them effectively against evidence, even though it is often there for them to use. So the enquiry/process skills have to be used scientifically if scientific ideas are to be developed. Hence the importance of taking action to help the development of these skills (see Module 2).

Activity 2

The enquiry framework is further applied here in relation to either, or both, of the two vignettes. Try to work on both before comparing your findings with what one group of teachers produced for 'Gavin and the Coke can' (Figure 1.7). This group showed two 'rounds' of the cycle of events, representing the first trial and the attempt of Gavin's group to cling on to the initial idea by invoking something that could not be seen, and the second trial where they could not avoid recognising that their idea did not really explain the situation. There

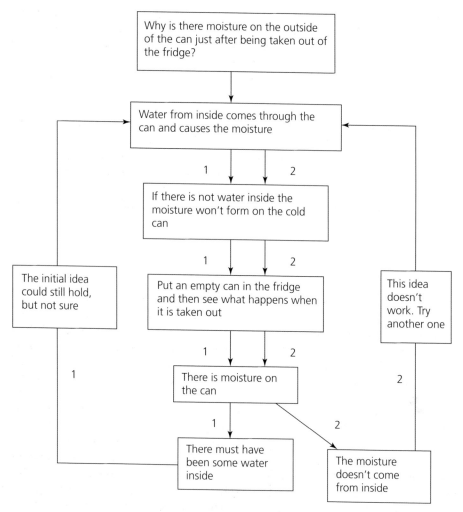

Figure 1.7 Gavin's enquiry

would probably be a third round also, when the idea that came up from discussion in the second round (the communication and reflection box to the right) was tested. Figure 1.7 illustrates that there are cycles of enquiry in a single investigation; sometimes a cycle is conducted very quickly (even in thought rather than in action in some cases) and sometime it is slow, as in the case of Emma and the seeds, where the ideas were tested over a long time scale.

The framework suggests that the essential process/enquiry skills that are used are: raising questions, predicting, planning, gathering evidence by observing and measuring, interpreting evidence and drawing conclusions and communicating and reflecting critically. While these can be expressed in different ways – and various terms are sometimes used – they describe the important steps in the enquiry process.

The vignettes also draw attention to the role of the ideas that children bring to the activity. Their predictions are based on these ideas. Research into children's ideas shows that they are firmly held. The implications of this will be taken up in discussion of the next activity.

First, however, bringing together the points made about learning through enquiry we arrive at a possible definition:

> Learning through enquiry means building understanding by testing one's own and others' ideas through gathering evidence from direct experience, from books and other resources including computer-based ones, from the teacher, and from other informed adults. As a result, the idea tested may be found not to fit the evidence, in which case an alternative one has to be tried, or the idea may be found to fit, in which case it is extended in its application and becomes a little 'bigger'.

Activity 3

The description of how Emma and Gavin used their pre-existing ideas to make sense of their experiences draws attention to the role of these ideas in children's learning. Activity 3 asks you to look at some ideas that children often hold. All of these come from research and have been found frequently; they are not idiosyncratic and untypical of children's thinking. As you read them you may well be able to sympathise with the children who hold these ideas, for they seem reasonable given the children's likely experiences. As with other of children's ideas (some reported by Osborne and Freyberg, 1985, and others in the SPACE research reports), they are a mixture of partially formed scientific ideas and what we might call 'everyday' ideas. There are plenty of 'everyday' ideas for children to pick up, for we use scientific names and concepts very loosely and often use words metaphorically. Children will not realise this when, for instance, they hear people refer to a fire as 'alive' or to giving plants 'food'. In daily talk we generally mean small plants when we speak of garden plants, and refer to trees and bushes by other names. We see notices that say 'no animals allowed' where this only refers to non-human animals. All these create understandings that are in conflict with scientific language. The children do not realise that some words have precise meanings in science although are used more loosely in other contexts.

Children's limited experience can lead them to ideas that seem strange, until we realise that they are consistent with some evidence available to the children. For example, they may well have seen rust seemingly emerging from the inside of metal, for example when painted iron railings become rusted under the paint, which then flakes off to reveal the rust. And the sensation of 'seeing' is of directing our eyes towards what is seen, so it may seem that the eyes are active in 'doing the seeing' and need to be switched on.

In all the examples of ideas there is evidence of the children working things out from their observations, not just making up the ideas without reason.

Research also shows that they make sense to the children and so they will hold on to these ideas if no other more reasonable explanation is available to them. Even when they are introduced to the 'correct' explanation, this often makes less sense to them than their own idea. So it is important to ensure that their idea is tested because until it is shown to be less useful than an alternative one, they will still believe it.

This argues for taking children's own ideas seriously and enabling them to see the evidence for themselves that requires a change in their view or suggests that an alternative explanation should be tried. This is one way of helping children to move towards more scientific ideas. The characteristics of children's ideas provide some clues as to how we might change their ideas (see Module 2). So, for example, if an idea seems to be based on limited experience, more can be given, chosen to challenge the child's idea – such as by cutting a rusty nail and showing that there is shiny metal inside but rust only on the outside.

Activity 4

Some ways of accessing children's ideas can be inferred from the examples given in Activity 3. Clearly asking children directly what they think can be effective, but it is necessary to put the question in the right form (see Module 3). Drawings can also be useful for young children, particularly if annotated by the teacher in discussion with the child. Other approaches that teachers use are

- children discussing in groups, with the teacher listening
- drawings and strip cartoon of changes in objects or events
- Writing down predictions and explanations of particular situations
- annotating drawings
- concept maps
- concept cartoons.

Some of these are shown in the examples in Module 8 which is concerned with formative assessment (assessment for learning). Finding out children's ideas is the first step in using assessment to help learning when a constructivist approach is taken to learning. This underlines that formative assessment is part of teaching and not a separate activity.

REFERENCES

ASE (1998) *Primary Science*, No. 56, Hatfield: Association for Science Education.
Hawking, S.W. (1988) *A Brief History of Time*, London: Bantam Press.

FURTHER READING

Harlen, W. (2001) *Primary Science: Taking the Plunge*, 2nd edn, Portsmouth, NH: Heinemann.

Harlen, W. and Jelly, S. (1997) 'Why this way of working?', *Developing Science in the Primary Classroom*, Chapter 4, Harlow: Longman.

Osborne, R.J. and Freyberg, P. (1985) *Learning in Science: The Implications of Children's Science*, London: Heinemann.

SPACE Project Research Report (1990) *Light*, Liverpool: Liverpool University Press.

SPACE Project Research Report (1992) *Processes of Life*, Liverpool: Liverpool University Press.

Module 2 The teacher's role in promoting progress

INTRODUCTION

This module is concerned with identifying ways of enabling development towards scientific understanding at an appropriate level. Children acquire and develop ideas informally, through everyday experience. In Module 1, consideration was given to the importance of children's own interpretations of their observations. In a formal classroom setting, not only can children's understanding be explored and extended but, as discussions and interpretations of their experiences progress, between teacher and children and between children themselves, so possibilities for practical investigations can emerge.

Of course, as teachers (and 'experts'), the temptation could simply be to tell children where their ideas and explanations are flawed and that their ideas therefore need to change. This could be quickly and efficiently done by giving them 'answers' in the form of the 'correct' understanding, or as a definition or as a rule.

However, it is important to value the ideas that children express and to encourage them, not only to express and share these ideas, but also to try to explain their basis, or origin. Children's understanding is likely to change most effectively if they are encouraged to investigate further what they think they know and to test, for themselves, whether their ideas can be consistently applied. If children can be involved in planning their own investigations, they can be encouraged scientifically to conclude whether their ideas are valid, or if they should reformulate them.

Through the course of four activities, you will be considering ways of developing both the enquiry skills that were identified in the enquiry framework, in Module 1, and the ideas that children have.

Activity 1 comprises a series of tasks designed to identify enquiry skills in action. Each task predominantly exemplifies one skill. If you are working alone, there is no need to set out the equipment. The description of the tasks will be sufficient for you to identify the skill (shown in Figure 2.2) that is required. This is about confirming a definition of each skill. Now you go on to identify what it is that children are actually doing when they are engaged in an activity and using each particular skill. In Figure 2.3, you record characteristics of each of the six skills in the framework. Some real investigation might help you to do this and, if you are not actually involved in practical work, at this stage, you might want to find an opportunity to complete Figure 2.3 next time you are working with, or watching, children who are involved in an investigation. Activity 2 presents a vignette of a teacher introducing a 'Gardening' topic. Using a list of starting points that the children identified, you are invited to produce plans for activities that will enhance children's skills and identify strategies that they could deploy, to encourage the use of these skills. Figure 2.4 is provided for you to list such teaching strategies. Activity 3 turns to a consideration of children's ideas. Four examples are cited. You are invited to consider how you might respond to each of these ideas – whether to the child individually, or whether you use the ideas as the basis for a group discussion. As you consider positive or constructive responses, you are then asked to list possible reasons for or origins of children's own ideas. These reasons are categorised in Activity 4 and you are involved in describing teaching strategies that you could use in response to ideas in each category.

Activity 1

Task 1 Minibeasts

In each container there is a different animal. Note two similarities and two differences between them.

Task 2 Pea in a bottle

Hold a plastic bottle horizontally and put a pea inside the neck of the bottle. Hold the bottle level with your mouth and blow a short, sharp breath into the bottle. The result might surprise you, so repeat this experiment several times to be sure about what happens. Try to describe a reason that explains what you have seen happening. Devise tests for your explanation. Take care you do not choke by inhaling the pea!

Task 3 Water

One beaker contains sea water, the other tap water. What are the differences between them? Make a list of questions you might investigate.

Task 4 Pendulum

Plan an investigation to find out what affects the time taken for one swing of the pendulum.

Activity 1 *continued*

Task 5 Pulse rate

The line graph in Figure 2.1 shows a child's pulse rate during three different activities. The activities were writing, walking and skipping. Explain the shape of each line on the graph and decide which line represents which activity.

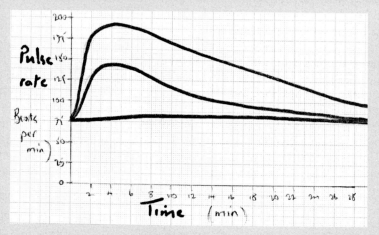

Figure 2.1 Child's pulse rate during three activities

Use the grid in Figure 2.2 to record the main skill required for each task. When you have completed the tasks, use Figure 2.3 to identify the main characteristics of each of these skills. One example is given for each skill.

	Raising questions	Predicting	Planning	Observing/ Measuring	Interpreting	Communicating/ Reflecting
Task 1						
Task 2						
Task 3						
Task 4						
Task 5						

Figure 2.2 Skills required in the five tasks

Activity 1 *continued*

> *Raising questions*: Asking a question that can be investigated
>
> *Predicting*: Using knowledge rather than guessing
>
> *Planning*: Identifying variables
>
> *Observing/Measuring*: Noting similarities
>
> *Interpreting*: Using data
>
> *Communicating/Reflecting*: Using graphs

Figure 2.3 Enquiry skills characteristics

Activity 2

Children were working on a 'Gardening' topic. In a discussion at the start of their work, children described their gardening experiences. Several reported success with projects growing flowers or vegetables. A few thought that 'gardening' was always about weeding. Some said that it is always too wet or windy to do much in the garden and most agreed that when the weather is sunny, it's usually too hot to bother gardening.

The class visited a market garden and another day they spent some time in a local park, studying trees. The idea of growing their own plants began to appeal to them and an area of the school ground was designated as theirs, to cultivate.

Some of the children who had gardened before volunteered to be an 'Expert Gardener' panel. The rest of the class asked the panel questions and shared ideas about gardening and growing things. The teacher took notes. Ideas were shared, views were expressed, questions were raised and activities were suggested. The teacher summarised these as 'Starting Points' for their topic work:

- Buy some flower seeds to germinate.
- Buy some vegetable seeds to germinate.
- Collect some fruit and/or vegetable seeds (tomato, cucumber, lemon, avocado) to germinate.
- Experimenting with a 'cloche' (old lemonade bottle).
- Collect and compare leaves from trees.
- Identify trees.
- Test different gardening gloves.
- Record weather conditions.
- Grow the tallest sunflower.
- Compare commercial composts.

Activity 2 *continued*

For each starting point:

- Outline a possible investigation.
- Identify the enquiry skill(s) being used.
- Describe what the children could actually do and how your intervention or encouragement would help to develop the skill(s).

Use Figure 2.4 to collate examples of teaching strategies that are useful for developing each skill.

SKILL	STRATEGY
Raising questions	
Predicting	
Planning	
Observing/Measuring	
Interpreting	
Communicating/Reflecting	

Figure 2.4 Examples of teaching strategies

Activity 3 *continued*

Read these examples of children's ideas. Describe how you would respond to each idea and why. When you have considered each idea, compile a list of possible reasons for or origins of children's ideas.

Evaporation

One child considered that clouds have an 'active' role in the process of evaporation:

> When the water evaporates, it goes on a cloud and then the cloud goes in any place and later it will go out as rain. It will keep going until it is all gone and then it will go to another place with water and do the same. The cloud is like a magnet so the water goes through the cracks and goes up, that is what I think.
>
> (SPACE Research Report, 1990a, p. 30)

Growing

Children collected some seeds to germinate. They put them in pots. The teacher asked the children what the seeds would need to grow well. Warmth, light and food were suggested. One child recorded: 'The seed will grow in the pot. The mud in the pot will get used up because that's where the food for the seed comes from. When it gets bigger we'll give it some plant food.'

Light

A 10 year old drew a picture to show how she sees the light from a candle.

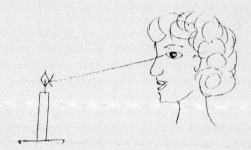

Figure 2.5 A child's idea of seeing

Source: SPACE Research Report (1990b, p. 24)

Forces

Some children, learning about forces and their effects, concluded that: 'The ball keeps rolling because there is a force pushing it. When it stops rolling there is no force on the ball' (adapted from Gunstone and Watts, 1985).

Activity 4

Figure 2.6 summarises the possible bases for the origin of children's ideas. For each one, define or exemplify teaching strategies to use, in response to children's ideas.

Basis of children's ideas	Response
Derived from limited experience	
Based on limited perceptions	
Focused on one feature, ignoring others	
A consequence of faulty reasoning	
Tied to a particular context	
Based on misunderstandings and everyday use of words	

Figure 2.6 Basis of children's ideas

Source: Harlen (2001, p. 61)

DISCUSSION AND REFLECTION

Activity 1

It is important to make the point that, although such tasks, individually, could be encountered or undertaken by primary children, it is not the intention here to suggest that you should offer such a series of tasks in a classroom. Rather, it is offered as a vehicle to focus on defining the characteristics of the set of enquiry skills we encountered in the enquiry framework in Module 1.

Task 1 involved observing. The main focus of task 2 is on predicting, but of course, if you actually tried this, you might have become involved in detailed planning, identifying a 'fair' way of controlling the blow each time, and then involved in a higher order of predicting by offering hypotheses for the behaviour of the pea. Task 3 begins with raising questions, but you could soon become involved in planning the detail of the comparative investigations that you identify in your questions. Task 4 requires a high order of planning skills and the plans, of course, derive from questions that you had to pose about changing the behaviour of the pendulum. Task 5 is about interpreting data that are presented on the graph.

If you are not familiar with the words used in the enquiry framework, you might have struggled with, for instance, identifying when a question becomes a prediction and what is the difference between hypothesising and interpreting. That is why the next part of the Activity asks that you complete Figure 2.3, by describing the characteristics (i.e. what it is that children will be doing, or might be encouraged to do) of each of the enquiry skills. A list of suggestions follows.

> *Raising questions*: Being inquisitive; asking questions that can be investigated; recognising questions that cannot; turning a question into an investigation; looking for answers
>
> *Predicting*: Applying knowledge and experience to attempt a prediction; justifying or explaining a prediction; using hypotheses to make predictions, rather than just guessing
>
> *Planning*: Making a plan that identifies variables; defining controls; deciding what to change, in an investigation; what to record; what to measure; selecting resources and equipment
>
> *Observing/Measuring*: Using the senses; describing; noting similarities; noting differences; comparing; sequencing; sorting
>
> *Interpreting*: Making conclusions from results; seeing patterns in data; using keys; generalising; inferring; using data; accepting alternative explanations
>
> *Communicating/Reflecting*: following instructions; describing; reporting; using tables, graphs and charts; listening

Figure 2.7 Enquiry skills characteristics

None of the tasks explicitly required the use of communicating or reflecting. You might like to ensure that you include opportunities and describe strategies for developing these skills in Activity 2.

Activity 2

A number of investigations will derive from children's questions about growing conditions (temperature, water, light, soil type, for example). If the rate of successful germination of seeds from different sources is to be compared, it is likely that children will want to provide their own seeds, too. Your role is first of all to steer the children's questions and ideas for investigations towards practicable enquiries. So, for example, if the 'best' conditions/seeds/soils are to be investigated, it is important that the tests have been fair so you will need to invite different groups studying these questions to ensure that their tests are controlled so that comparisons between the work of different groups are valid. The 'starting points' can all result in an investigation covering every step in the enquiry framework. The focus, here, is the teaching strategies to employ rather than the content of the investigations and the strategies described for each skill should be capable of developing the sorts of behaviour outlined in Figure 2.3.

When you think about the children you know, you will have recognised that some investigations will require more input from you than others. It is important to try to achieve a balance between your input and direction and opportunities for groups of children to share their own planning, in order that children retain some interest in and 'ownership' of their work.

You will have recognised, also, that it is in the nature of practical work involving growing plants, that there will be periods of apparent inactivity. Related activities, like recording weather patterns or 'consumer' testing (on gardening gloves, for example) can be useful for these periods.

Examples of strategies that teachers have identified as useful include

- *Raising questions*: If a topic is introduced with a 'brainstorm' or a mind-mapping exercise, try to harness the children's thinking by asking them what they would like to find out. Develop some of the ideas into investigable questions, such as: 'What happens if . . . ?', 'I wonder whether . . . ?', 'How can we . . . ?'
- *Predicting*: Show interest in a child's ideas; give time for them to be expressed and invite others to endorse or contest an idea. This can help to foster an environment in which 'forming' an idea is accepted. Ask: 'What do you think might happen . . . ?', 'Why do you think . . . ?'
- *Planning*: If a fair conclusion is to be drawn from an investigation, encourage the children to ask: 'What shall I keep the same?', 'What do we need to change?', 'What should we record?', 'Which changes shall I measure (and when and how)?', as they develop their plans.
- *Observing/Measuring*: When they are making comparisons and looking for similarities and differences, ask the children: 'What else did you notice?' Encourage the (safe) use of more than one skill: 'What did you smell?', 'How did it feel?'
- *Interpreting*: Encourage displays of the results of children's investigations, so that data (a table, chart or graph, for example) can form the basis of questions such as: 'What happened when . . . ?' or 'What would happen if . . . ?'
- *Communicating/Reflecting*: Arrange for children to report the outcomes of their investigations to different audiences; encourage the use of a variety of media for recording; require children to listen to the reports of others.

Activity 3

You might have thought that the children with whom you normally work are unlikely to have some of these ideas. However, the principle of the exercise is that your response is one in which the idea is respected. The examples here appear to have been written or drawn. If you captured such evidence in a conversation, your response, in principle, would be no different. You might invite the child, or a group, to consider applying the idea in a different context or you might be able to elicit different ideas from the group. If it were appropriate, you might be able to turn the idea into an investigable question, with the aim of either endorsing or challenging the idea. Children's ideas expressed by drawing can be compared, then discussed. If an investigation is difficult to arrange, it might be appropriate to introduce a different idea. Specific examples follow, for each of the four ideas.

Evaporation

One strategy would be to try to apply the idea in a different context. You could invite the child to explain whether clouds are involved in the evaporation of water from a saucer in the classroom. What happens if there are no clouds? A discussion of the phenomenon of evaporation with a group might elicit different ideas: 'The water just soaks in. It doesn't go up, it goes down.' What happens to the water on a saucer, left in a cupboard?

Growing

The nature of the 'food' needs might be considered. If the growing medium is 'consumed' by the plant, presumably there is a measurable change and children could devise an appropriate investigation. As before, you could try to apply the idea to a different context: 'Is the soil in the garden being used up? If so, does it get replaced?', 'Do all plants need soil to grow?' This might not be something that children have encountered, and, if there is a local pond to visit, this would provide an alternative experience. But then, some might counter, cut flowers in a vase of water don't live long!

Light

Ideas based on intuition could be challenged by an alternative suggestion: 'Do you think the light could be coming from the candle?' However, you are unlikely to change a child's understanding if there is no apparent (to the child) reason to do so. After all, if a child is frequently told to 'look closely' in order to 'see everything', the words convey a suggestion that seeing is 'active' and that the means to see (light) must come from us. You could ask the child why we can't see in the dark, but this is likely to be explicable, in terms of 'active seeing', by a notion that our eyes are 'switched on' to enable us to 'see'. Sunrise and sunset, with the gradual appearance and disappearance of light – and where that light comes from – would make an interesting basis for discussion.

Forces

Encouraging consistent use of language (even if it is not, at first, the usual scientific terminology) can help in interpreting different phenomena. A lot of experience with 'pushing' and 'pulling' and how things move will help to explain some aspects of forces and movement. However, in this example, the intuitive interpretation of the rolling ball is that there must be something (the 'force pushing') to keep it moving. In fact the child has identified momentum – but is unlikely to be helped by being told that! The contrasting behaviour of a ball rolling on flat ground and one rolling downhill might be considered. Why does one slow down and the other one speed up?

Different reasons have been offered for responding to the ideas in different ways. A summary follows, of the likely basis of a child's ideas:

- With only *limited experience,* a child who thinks that 'light things always float' can be encouraged to explore floating and sinking further.
- A *perception* that there is less water than there was ice or snow, before melting, is based only on looking.
- With a *restricted focus* on possible variables, during an investigation, a child might conclude that 'the smallest ball bounces best'.

- A lack of rigour can result in an idea based on *faulty reasoning*: water might pass through soil in less time than it takes to pass through stones, in a funnel, but the effect of clay binding the stones might have been overlooked.
- The influence of *context* – for example, indoors/outdoors – can affect the nature of an idea.
- The *common use of words* can cause ideas to be expressed in misleading ways: 'No animals allowed . . .' or 'The clouds will melt away . . .'

Activity 4

Figure 2.8 summarises a number of strategies to use, according to the likely basis of a child's idea.

Basis of children's ideas	Response
Derived from limited experience	Provide wider experience to challenge ideas: plants growing without soil; wood that doesn't float; hearing sound through water and solid material; light and heavy items falling through air at the same rate
Based on limited perceptions	Review the investigation; focus on the process of change, not just on the starting and ending conditions, leading to a different interpretation of the perception
Focused on one feature, ignoring others	Ask them to go on thinking: 'Anything else?' 'Would it be enough just to give the plant water?'
A consequence of faulty reasoning	Help children to test their ideas more rigorously (fairly) and to use all the evidence in drawing a conclusion: 'Was each one measured for the same length of time, with the same amount of water?'
Tied to a particular context	Encourage them to apply the idea in a different but related context to see if it still 'works': 'Can the idea that water condenses from the air explain the moisture on cold cans taken out of the fridge?'
Based on misunderstandings and everyday use of words	Ask them for examples of what they mean and introduce scientific terms alongside the ones children use, for example 'see-through' or 'transparent'; 'melting' or 'dissolving'

Figure 2.8 Summary of appropriate outcomes

REFERENCES

Driver, R., Guesne, E. and Tiberghien, A. (eds) (1985) *Children's Ideas in Science*, Milton Keynes: Open University Press.

Gunstone, R. and Watts, M. (1985) 'Force and motion', in R. Driver, E. Guesne and A. Tiberghien (eds) *Children's Ideas in Science*, Milton Keynes: Open University Press.

Harlen, W. (2001) *Primary Science: Taking the Plunge*, Portsmouth, NH: Heinemann.

SPACE Research Report (1990a) *Evaporation and Condensation*, Liverpool: Liverpool University Press.

SPACE Research Report (1990b) *Light*, Liverpool: Liverpool University Press.

Module 3 Teachers' questions and responses to children's questions

INTRODUCTION

This module is concerned with the role of questions in learning and teaching through enquiry. It concerns both the questions that teachers ask and the questions that children ask. In relation to the former we are concerned with the questions that help children to express their ideas, so that teachers can take these into account, and with the questions that promote children to use and develop enquiry skills. In relation to children's questions, we consider their value in learning and thus the importance of encouraging questioning and, conversely, not discouraging it by the kind of response, or non-response, given. Primary teachers often find difficulty in knowing how to answer questions that require scientific understanding that is beyond the children and so particular attention is given to how to deal with this type of question.

Teachers ask questions for a variety of purposes: to provoke children's thinking, to find out what children's ideas are, to monitor and regulate progress in an activity, to control behaviour, to check on understanding. Our concern here is with those particular questions that help teachers to find out about children's thinking and that encourage them to use enquiry skills. We look at the most effective ways of framing questions for these purposes.

The relationship between the wording and the effect of teachers' questions has led to various ways of categorising questions. For example, Sheila Jelly (2001) divided teachers' questions into 'productive' and 'unproductive' (of scientific activity), while Jos Elstgeest, in the same book (*Primary Science: Taking the Plunge*, 2001), distinguished between different kinds of 'productive' questions. He identified 'attention-focusing questions', 'measuring and counting questions', 'comparison questions', 'action questions' and 'problem-posing questions'. He pointed out that teachers not only need to know the difference between these but also to recognise when particular kinds of questions are appropriate.

By paying attention to the wording and timing of questions teachers can effectively promote learning through enquiry or alternatively discourage it, if the wrong questions are asked or are asked at the wrong time (see Elstgeest 2001). So in Activity 1 we look at questions that are effective in eliciting children's ideas by encouraging them to explain how they make sense of some event or situation. This activity involves you in creating some questions and then classifying them. This is best carried out in a group with others. However, in the Discussion and Reflection section, an alternative is suggested that will enable you to engage in the same kind of thinking even though you may be working alone. Activity 2 concerns questions that teachers ask to encourage children to use enquiry skills. Together these first activities help to identify the wording of questions that can be used to advance children's thinking.

We consider children's questions and how to handle them in the second part of the module. In science we are concerned with questions about the 'what, how and why' of things around us. The answers that we have to these questions come from people who have investigated and collected evidence to test their ideas. So the most useful questions that children ask are those that lead to investigations from which they can find things out for themselves. When children realise that they can do this, they have made a good start in their scientific development. They also have to realise that some questions cannot be answered by science. So it is necessary in responding to children's questions to make clear the kinds of questions that can be answered by scientific enquiry. This is helped by giving the children the opportunity to investigate and answer their own questions.

Children's questions are important to their learning because it is often through asking questions that they make the link between one experience and another and so develop broader and 'bigger' ideas (see Module 1). Their questions can also give the teacher information about what the children are struggling to understand. So we need to encourage questioning and particularly, in science, the questions that can be answered by scientific enquiry. But this means that the teacher has to be able to deal with the questions effectively, otherwise children will be discouraged from questioning. Activity 3 presents a way of categorising questions that children ask, as a first step to considering how to handle questions of different kinds. One of these categories of questions is the most difficult to deal with because to answer them would require complex scientific concepts beyond the understanding of primary school children. Activity 4 introduces a way of handling these questions without attempting to answer them directly.

In both asking questions and encouraging children to ask questions, it is not enough to pay attention to framing and categorising questions. The classroom climate has a significant part to play as well. First, there is the social climate. Children must feel 'safe' to express their ideas in answering questions and in raising questions themselves. They must not be made to feel that their answers or questions are 'silly'. Otherwise they will soon stop expressing them. So the teacher must accept all answers and questions as valuable and treat them seriously. It may be necessary to ask children to explain their questions or answers if they do not seem sensible at first. Children must also respect each others' comments and the teacher's example will be important here.

Then there is the physical environment which can also be made to encourage questioning and thinking. This is created by, for example, having displays that provide the opportunity to explore materials and interesting objects brought in by the teacher or children, with relevant reference books and sometimes cards inviting careful observation or questions at hand. A question box near to such a display enables children to pose questions at any time. The teacher might announce a time when questions will be discussed. In responding, the categorisation suggested in Activity 3 can be applied.

Activity 1

Watch the demonstration of the Cartesian diver (see Discussion and Reflection section if you are working alone). Suppose you are showing this to children and want to find out the children's ideas on how it works. What questions would you ask the children? Write down two questions on separate slips of paper (don't put your name on them). Work out and put down the exact words that you would use, not just indications of the questions.

Activity 2

Consider this scenario:

During a period of cold weather with snow and ice on the roads, children ask why there is salt on the road. So at a convenient time the teacher provides the equipment for them to investigate the melting of ice in fresh water and in salt water. The teacher wants them to make predictions, then test these with fair tests, make relevant measurements, interpret what they find and then see if this affects their ideas about the difference the salt makes.

During the various stages of the investigation, what questions would the teacher ask in order to encourage children to use and develop their enquiry skills? Working in pairs, write down some questions for each of the skills, using the wording you think is most effective. Complete Figure 3.1.

Activity 2 *continued*

Enquiry skill	Teacher's questions
Raising questions	
Predicting	
Planning an investigation	
Gathering evidence by observing and measuring	
Interpreting evidence	
Communicating and reflecting	

Figure 3.1 Pro-forma: developing enquiry skills

Categorisation of children's questions

Types of question (illustrated by questions asked when a bird's nest was brought into a classroom):

(a) Questions that are really comments expressed as questions ('Why are birds so clever that they can weave nests with their beaks?').

(b) Questions requiring simple factual answers ('Where was the bird's nest found?').

(c) Questions requiring more complex answers ('Why do some birds nest in trees and some on the ground?').

(d) Questions that lead to enquiry by the child ('What is the nest made of?').

(e) Philosophical questions ('Why are birds made so that they can fly and not other animals?').

Activity 3

Here are some questions asked by children during observation of tadpoles in an aquarium:

1 Why are they called tadpoles?
2 Are they fish?
3 What do they eat?
4 Can they see me?
5 Will they turn into frogs?
6 What do they feel like?
7 Why does the surface of the water look shiny when you look from underneath?
8 How old are they?
9 Why are they so wriggly?
10 Why do some things turn into something else, like caterpillars turning into butterflies?

Try to categorise the questions into the categories (a) to (e) or some other category that you suggest (see Figure 3.2). Then consider what you as a teacher would do, to enable the children to have an answer to each question.

Question	Category	How to handle the question
1		
2		
3		
4		
5		
6		
7		
8		
9		
10		

Figure 3.2 Handling questions

'Turning' questions into investigable ones

While encouraging children to ask questions of all kinds is important to children's learning, in science it is particularly valuable to help children to ask questions that they can answer through enquiry. Some questions of this kind (category (d)) are ones that they can straightaway answer for themselves by their own actions. More difficult to handle are the ones that require complex answers.

In a chapter on questioning in *Primary Science: Taking the Plunge* Sheila Jelly (2001) suggests a way of 'turning questions' of a complex kind into ones that are more easily investigated by children:

> Essentially it is a strategy for handling complex questions and in particular those of the 'why' kind that are the most frequent of all spontaneous questions. They are difficult questions because they carry an apparent request for a full explanation which may not be known to the teacher and, in any case, is likely to be conceptually beyond a child's understanding.
>
> The strategy recommended is one that turns the question to practical action with a 'let's see what we can do to understand more' approach. The teaching skill involved is the ability to 'turn' the question. Consider, for example, a situation in which children are exploring the properties of fabrics. They have dropped water on different types and become fascinated by the fact that water stays 'like a little ball' on felt. They tilt the felt, rolling the ball around, and someone asks 'Why is it like a ball?' How might the question be turned by applying the 'doing more to understand' approach? We need to analyze the situation quickly and use what I call a 'variables scan'. The explanation must relate to something 'going on' between the water and the felt surface so causing the ball. That being so, ideas for children's activities will come if we consider ways in which the situation could be varied to better understand the making of the ball. We could explore surfaces keeping the drop the same, and explore drops keeping the surface the same. These thoughts can prompt others that bring ideas nearer to what children might do. For example:
>
> 1   Focusing on the surface, keeping the drop the same:
>   What is special about the felt that helps make the ball? Which fabrics are good 'ball-makers'?
>   Which are poor?
>   What have the good ball-making fabrics in common? What surfaces are good ball-makers?
>   What properties do these share with the good ball-making fabrics?
>   Can we turn the felt into a poor ball-maker?
> 2   Focusing on the water drop, keeping the surface the same:
>   Are all fluids good ball-makers?
>   Can we turn the water into a poor ball-maker?

Notice how the 'variables scan' results in the development of productive questions that can be explored by the children. The original question has been turned to practical activity and children exploring along these lines will certainly enlarge their understanding of what is involved in the phenomenon. They will not arrive at a detailed explanation but may be led towards simple generalization of their experience, such as 'A ball will form when . . .' or 'It will not form when . . .'.

(Jelly, 2001, p. 45)

Activity 4

Try the variables scan approach to question 7 in the list considered in Activity 3. Suggest other general approaches to the different kinds of questions that teachers can take to ensure that children find answers to their questions.

DISCUSSION AND REFLECTION

Activity 1

Even if you are working alone and therefore do not have a demonstration to watch, it is useful to focus on a particular event for this activity. A Cartesian diver is easily set up. You need a 2-litre clear plastic drinks bottle and a dropper (a glass file with a rubber bulb, as used for eye or nose-drops). Almost fill the bottle with water. Weight the dropper with plasticine and put it into the bottle. Adjust the weighting so that the dropper floats upright. Put the top on the bottle and squeeze the sides. The 'diver' should sink when pressure is put on the bottle sides and rise again when released. You may need to adjust the plasticine and make sure that there is only a little water in the glass file when the sides are not squeezed.

Write down several questions that you would ask children (exact wording) to find out what ideas they have about how this works.

Then look at questions other teachers have suggested in Figure 3.3. They have been arranged in four groups. What do you notice that is similar about the questions in each group? Remember that the intention was to get the children to explain their ideas about how the diver works. So even though set C are useful questions (and of the kind we will consider in Activity 2), they are not eliciting the children's ideas. The relevant features of the questions in each group are:

- Set A questions are described as 'subject-centred' (i.e. they ask, What is happening?, Why does the diver go down?).
- Set B questions are described as 'person-centred' (i.e. they ask, What do you think . . . ?, the emphasis is on the 'you').

Set A	Set B
Why does the diver go down when you squeeze the bottle? What does squeezing do? Can you explain what is happening here? What is the reason for the diver rising when the sides are released?	How do you explain what makes the diver go down? What do you think squeezing does that makes the diver sink? Explain why you think the diver goes up again when you stop squeezing. What do you think is causing the diver to sink when you squeeze the bottle?
Set C	Set D
What do you think would happen if you squeeze very hard? Where else have you noticed something like this? What do you see happening inside the diver when it goes down? Can you show me how to make the diver stay at the bottom? Can you make it float half-way down?	Does the diver go down more quickly if you squeeze harder? Which way does it move when you release the bottle? Does the squeezing make the water go up in the glass file?

Figure 3.3 Teachers' questions on the Cartesian diver

- Set C questions are asking for processes not explanations (What did you notice?, What do you think will happen if . . . ?). These are considered in Activity 2.
- Set D questions are closed, requiring perhaps single word answers (Will the diver go down more quickly or more slowly if you press harder?, Did you expect that to happen?).

Set B, the 'person-centred' questions, are the ones that invite the children to give their ideas and are important for 'starting from children's ideas'. The significant features of these questions are:

- They demonstrate interest in the children's ideas (the important emphasis on 'what *you* think').
- They don't ask for a 'right' answer.
- They can be answered by all children even if they realise they don't know the reason, but they have their ideas.

By contrast, the subject-centred questions indicate that there is a 'right' answer and children who do not know it will not be able to provide an answer to the question (and the teacher loses the opportunity to know what the children are thinking).

Both person- and subject-centred questions can in theory be 'open' or 'closed' but in practice most of the person-centred questions are open and more of the subject-centred ones are closed.

In the light of this discussion you may like to rephrase one or two of the questions that you wrote down about the diver.

Activity 2

Although it is obvious that to encourage a child to use a particular enquiry skill, you ask a question that requires its use as a response, it is not always easy to do this in practice. To see if you are on the right lines, you might like to read through some examples of questions asked in a different context.

Scenario: Children are exploring a collection of dry seeds before planting them. The children then plant them in various conditions, which the teacher wants them to decide for themselves. They predict what will happen in different situations. As the seeds germinate and the plants grow, the children observe, measure and discuss the growth. They look at the results and see whether these are what they expected.

A question the teacher might ask

- To encourage children to raise questions: *What would you like to know about these seeds?*
- To encourage them to make predictions: *What do you think will happen to these seeds if you give them more water than those others?*
- To encourage planning: *What will you need to do to see if your idea about the temperature making the seeds grow more quickly is right?*
- To encourage data collection when the plants have grown: *How many of the seeds of each kind are growing? How much do they grow in a week?*
- To encourage interpretation: *Was there any connection between the size of the seed and how big the plant is? How does this compare with what you thought would happen?*
- To encourage communication and reflection: *What is the best way to show the others what you found? How could you improve your investigation to be more sure of the result?*

Activity 3

As noted in the Introduction, children's questions in science can be a source of anxiety to primary teachers, so you may be relieved to know that it is often not the best thing to attempt a straightforward answer to a child's question. This is because if they do not understand the answers, they may be put off from asking questions. Also, to give answers to questions when children could find the answers for themselves prevents them from 'learning how to learn'. It all depends on the question and that is why it is helpful to give attention to the kind of question before deciding how to handle it. We use the word 'handle' rather than 'answer' to indicate the difference between using the question to help children's learning and giving them information.

Question	Category	How to handle
Why are they called tadpoles?	(b) or possibly (e)	It's the name given to the stage before they turn into frogs but don't know why this particular name
Are they fish?	(b)	No, although they live like fish at the moment they will turn into frogs and then they can't live all the time in water
What do they eat?	(d)	That's something you could find out. Can you suggest how?
Can they see me?	(d)	We could try to find out. How would you do that?
Will they turn into frogs?	(b) and (d)	Yes. If we can keep them in the right way you will see that for yourself
What do they feel like?	(b) but perhaps (a)	It's best not to try to touch them; what do you think they would feel like?
Why does the surface of the water look shiny when you look from underneath?	(c)	See Activity 4
How old are they?	(b) or (d)	If known, say when they hatched. If not known – the children could find that out from a book (or Internet)
Why are they so wriggly?	(a)	They are always moving, aren't they?
Why do some creatures turn into something else, like caterpillars turn into butterflies?	(e) or could be (c) (needs to be clarified)	If (e) this isn't something we know or can find out

Figure 3.4 Categorisation of questions

You might like to compare your categorisation of the ten questions with these given by some teachers (see Figure 3.4).

Activity 4

The extract by Sheila Jelly outlines a method of handling those questions that appear to present the greatest difficulty. These questions require complex answers, not factual ones, and on the face of it they cannot be investigated by children. The idea of turning these questions into ones that children can investigate is useful to study and practise. It can transform a question that seems to present a problem into an opportunity for children to investigate.

Although this approach does not provide the child with an answer to the initial question, it does take the child's question seriously and leads to some worthwhile investigation. Some questions of this type are very close to the 'comments expressed as questions category' and a young child might easily have meant, by question 7, 'look at how shiny the surface looks from underneath!' However, if the child persists in asking 'Why does it look shiny?', then a 'Yes, that's interesting' reply will not be sufficient. The phenomenon could then be investigated, through looking at the surface from various angles. The children could hold an object above the water and see whether they can see it from underneath and try moving it to various places. The investigation could be extended to a thick block or sheet of glass, when surfaces can look like mirrors from some angles. For your own information you may like to know that the phenomenon is the result of the bending of light at the surface between water (or glass) and air. Light coming from an object close to the surface inside the water or glass cannot escape and is reflected. An eye placed below the surface but close to it will see this reflected light, not light coming through the surface. (If you find this difficult, then this is the reason for not attempting to explain it directly to children!)

Look back now at the types of questions discussed in Activity 3 and see if you can match a general approach to a type of question. If so, even if this is very rough, you have a way of handling questions of different kinds if you first recognise the category that they fall into. It is often necessary to ask the children to clarify their question. Sometimes this results in them realising for themselves how to answer it. Nor should we read too much into the particular words children use and conclude that 'why' questions always require explanations of a certain kind. For example, a child who at first asked 'Why does the tadpole turn into a frog?', then immediately said 'I mean, how does it happen?'. This is a question he was able to answer by observation. Children do not always frame their questions in terms of the kind of answer they want and it pays to probe a little to find the nature of their questions before deciding how to handle them.

REFERENCES

Elstgeest, J. (2001) 'The right question at the right time', in W. Harlen (ed.) *Primary Science: Taking the Plunge*, 2nd edn, Portsmouth, NH: Heinemann.

Jelly, S. J. (2001) 'Helping children raise questions – and answering them', in W. Harlen (ed.) *Primary Science: Taking the Plunge*, 2nd edn, Portsmouth, NH: Heinemann.

Module 4 Managing practical work in the classroom

INTRODUCTION

This module is about managing and organising practical science in primary classrooms. The activities focus on:

- identifying and evaluating aspects of good practice in relation to the management of lessons;
- organising lessons and deciding which type of practical work would be the most appropriate in order to meet learning objectives;
- storing and using equipment.

There are many ways of organising science in the primary classroom. The age of the children influences the management of the lesson. The very young children need to have a wide range of practical activities within one teaching session and the teacher's role is quite different from that of a teacher of 11 year olds. The content of the lesson and the learning objectives will also influence the way in which the lesson is organised. If you were teaching 4 year olds how to observe living things carefully and sensitively, you would probably make sure that each small group of children was with a knowledgeable adult or you would organise the teaching session so that you worked with one group at a time, while other children concentrated on activities which were less teacher intensive. Yet, if you were investigating how shadows were formed, you would probably make use of a sunny period and take all the children out onto the playground at the same time. Some teachers make use of support staff and parent helpers so that they can help the younger children to stay on task and, if this is the case, then it is the teacher's responsibility to plan for and manage the work of the helpers.

An important element of teaching practical science is for children to have time to express their own ideas and raise their own questions. Teaching is managed so that there is time to do this and time for children to reflect on what they have learned.

In Activity 1 there is an opportunity to consider the various parts of a lesson. You are asked to view video material of a teacher in the classroom and to think about how the teacher shares the learning objectives with the children, how the subject matter is introduced, the timing and pace of the lesson and the way in which the teacher manages to find out the children's ideas. There are many videos available which would suit your purpose. Some LEAs produce them and there is one available from the SCIcentre www.le.ac.uk/se/centres/sci/SCIcentre *Classroom Organisation for Primary Science*. Alternatively, you could video a short sequence in a local primary school. You will need to watch how the children react to questioning, how they work together in groups and how the resources are collected and used. There is an observational schedule for you to use but you may want to add items to the schedule if you think that any aspects of good teaching have been omitted. You will consider how the teacher handles any misconceptions which are shown and how the lesson is organised so that the skills of science can be practised and developed.

Activity 2 is about organising lessons. There are various types of practical work and you will find a discussion about these. You are asked to consider at least one of the stages in the medium-term plan which has been prepared by a trainee teacher. You will need to think about how you would manage the activities so that the learning objectives can be met. Think about the way in which the content is introduced and how the children can be encouraged to make decisions and think about the science ideas. You will also consider how children might be provided with opportunities to plan in order to answer any questions which have been raised. It is hoped that if you are working with colleagues, that you will discuss the teacher's role and think about what he or she would be doing at every stage of the lesson.

In Activity 3 the focus is on the work of the very young children. The organisation is very different for this age group as much of their learning is through play. The management of the learning experiences is very complex and the science-based learning is integrated very closely with learning in other curriculum areas. If a focused task is planned, this will usually be done with four or five children and so it might take a week for all of the children in a class to have the opportunity to carry out the task. In some schools, the very young children are allowed to have a free choice about where they work and so they might choose not to visit the adult who is managing the focused task. Discuss with colleagues how you would react to this situation. Would you record the names of the children who had been involved and make notes about their learning, or would you try to arrange for every child to carry out the task?

The child-initiated learning will stem from the resources provided by the teacher and the dialogue which the teacher has with the children as they play. You are asked to think about some experiences which a teacher has planned for a class of 3- and 4-year-old children and to consider how these might be managed. Some of the activities might be available every day as part of the continuous provision and some activities you might want to carry out in a whole class group. Some of the activities use the same resources. There is a pro-forma for you to complete as you think about how you would organise the work.

Activity 4 concerns the management of resources. You are asked to think about those resources for scientific enquiry which you think should be in every classroom and those which need to be stored centrally. When you are thinking about the work of nursery classes and kindergartens you will need to consider whether they need a wider range of resources available at all times so that they can explore and play freely. You may like to draw on your own experience of storage systems and resource management in order to suggest a workable arrangement.

MANAGING THE ACTIVITIES

There is no single way to organise science in the primary classroom. How the teacher manages the activities will depend on the following:

- the nature of the task and the subject matter which is being studied;
- the resources available;
- the age of the children;
- the ancillary help which is available.

EVALUATING CLASSROOM MANAGEMENT

Although many schools use government or local schemes of work in order to plan their teaching, the way in which the lessons are organised depends on the space available, the learning styles of the children as well as the preferred teaching style of the teacher. What is important is that the children develop the appropriate attitudes to science and that they make progress in their scientific skills and their understanding of concepts. Practical work is enjoyable and children are usually highly motivated when they handle materials and equipment but there is no doubt that it makes many demands on teachers. It is much easier to begin a lesson by giving the children information, to go on to do a demonstration and then to ask the children to write an account of what has been done and what they have learned. Some children might learn by this method but they would not be developing their own process skills, the skills of scientific enquiry, and they would not be very enthusiastic about science.

In order to plan for practical work for a class of thirty children, the teacher has to collect equipment and resources. He or she also has to deal with the excitement which is often generated by practical investigation. However, the effort is worthwhile if children develop a sense of wonder as they begin to learn science ideas and begin to be able to plan investigations for themselves. It is surprising how quickly children begin to be independent and become able to collect and tidy away their own resources.

Activity 1 Evaluating classsroom management

Consider the features of good practice in primary science teaching which are listed on the observation schedule (see Figure 4.1) and then watch a video sequence of a teacher in the classroom. Naturally, what you can note about the teaching strategies will depend on the nature of the lesson which you are watching, but note the evidence that shows how the teacher is developing good practice. The purpose of this activity is not to be judgemental about a particular teacher but to emphasise the positive aspects of good management (see also Module 16).

Features of good teaching	Comments and examples
Were lesson objectives shared?	
How did the teacher introduce the activity? Was there reference to children's earlier work? Is the work related to children's own experiences?	
Were the children engaged in scientific enquiry? Were they raising questions, predicting, planning, gathering evidence by observing and measuring, interpreting evidence and drawing conclusions? Were they communicating and reflecting critically?	
Did you notice how the teacher helped the children in the development of science skills?	
Were there opportunities for children to express their ideas? Were children involved in planning their own investigations?	

Activity 1 *continued*

Features of good teaching	Comments and examples
Were all resources ready and well prepared? Were the resources suitable for the task?	
Was there any evidence of the teacher handling any misconceptions?	
Did the teacher find time to talk to all the groups? Is this necessary? Were any support staff used? Did they seem to be adequately prepared?	
Did any of the children say or do anything which would help the teacher to assess their understanding?	
Did the children enjoy their lesson? Did the teacher show enthusiasm?	

Figure 4.1 Observation schedule

Organising lessons

If we consider that children have their own ideas about science and that we have to build on their ideas when we organise practical work (see Module 1), then we have to consider how to organise the teaching so that there are opportunities for children to express these ideas. We have to be prepared to help them to modify their ideas if there is evidence of misconceptions. We also have to be aware of the fact that, in order to develop the skills of science, then we have to give children practice in planning their own practical investigations based on questions which they have raised.

In order to provide children with opportunities to develop both skills and understanding we may have to organise the practical work in a variety of ways. Sometimes you may want to start off with a demonstration which might get children thinking about ideas which they want to test out. Suppose that you poured some hot water into a clear beaker and into this you stirred some sugar, you would probably then ask the children where they thought the sugar had gone. You would collect their ideas about dissolving and perhaps help them to raise some questions which they would want to investigate for themselves. These might be about the size of sugar granules, the effect of the temperature of the water or the number of times the liquid was stirred. In this case you would be using the demonstration as a starting point for thinking. There are occasions when you will want to illustrate a particular concept and you might, in this case, ask the children to carry out an investigation which you had planned. The illustration might then lead to the children planning their own investigation in a subsequent lesson. If, for instance, you were teaching some 11 year olds about gases and you wanted them to observe the effects of carbon dioxide being given off by a mixture of yeast, warm milk and sugar, then you might give children instructions on how to combine the substances in a bottle and ask them to put the bottle in a warm place with a balloon over the neck of the bottle. The children would be practically involved but they would not be developing their own scientific skills. The purpose of the practical science in the lesson would be to stimulate thinking. The children could then go on to investigate questions which they raised themselves. These could be to do with the liquid in the bottle, the differences between dried and fresh yeast or the temperature of the liquid. There may be other occasions when the actual concepts are less important to the learning outcomes than the development of skills. For instance, you might want children to learn to use a particular piece of apparatus or to practise interpreting graphs. Teachers are clear about the learning outcomes of their lessons and they plan to manage the practical work in a way which best serves their purpose.

Activity 2

Look at the medium-term plan for a class of 6 year olds in Figure 4.2. These were prepared by a trainee teacher. The learning outcomes are identified as are the activities which the teacher wants to carry out. Think about how you would manage the practical work. Select a 'stage' and consider the following questions:

- Would the experiences take place over one or two weeks?
- Would you have all of the children doing the same thing at the same time?
- Would you have some children carrying out an activity while others were engaged on unrelated tasks?

Activity 2 continued

- What would the teacher do? Would he or she be with one group in order to find out their ideas and help them to develop skills or would he or she circulate and talk to as many children as possible? Would there be times when he or she would want to do a demonstration or even have all the children carrying out an investigation which he or she has planned?
- Would the children move around from one activity to another?
- How would you introduce and end the lessons?

Science class 1E 4 lessons 1hr 30 mins each week		
Learning objectives	Learning experiences	Resources and cross-curricular links
Stage 1 • Children will understand the meaning of the word 'transport' • Children understand that there are many forms of transport • Modes of transport can be classified • To observe carefully and to describe what they notice	Introduce topic by asking children: (a) How do they get to school? Is it by bus, car, or do they walk? Do they come in a train, an aeroplane or a boat? (b) When do they go in trains, boats, cars, aeroplanes, etc.? (c) Show pictures of helicopters/ gliders/aeroplanes/hot air balloons – do they move through air, sea or along the land? (d) Children to use storyboard to classify pictures of transport (Low Attainers) (e) or sorting circles (Middle Attainers), then draw large pictures or fill in sheet with drawings (Higher Attainers) to show which modes of transport travel through air, sea or land. Make autogyros or parachutes (or perhaps land yachts or boats) and describe how they fall and move.	• Pictures of heli-copters, gliders, etc. for sorting on storyboard • Smaller pictures for sorting circles • Frame for children to use for classification • Materials for making autogyros Cross-curricular links English – speaking and listening Mathematics – sorting into sets *Vocabulary* Helicopter, glider, hot air balloon, car, aeroplane, train, tractor, lorry, boat, ship, raft
Stage 2 Children will understand that: • There are many sorts of movement which can be described in many ways • Children will observe and describe different ways of moving • Children will recognise hazards in some moving objects	A *Children in circle on carpet* Link to last week's lesson on transport • How does a bus move? – on wheels • How does a car move?– on wheels • How does a train move? – on wheels • Show a toy car – child to move it – the wheels *rolled*.	• Pendulum to show swinging • Ball • Block and board to show sliding • Empty Coke bottle • Spinning top • Autogyros • Bubbles (floating in the air?) • Toy car/ramp

Activity 2 *continued*

Science class 1E 4 lessons 1hr 30 mins each week		
Learning objectives	Learning experiences	Resources and cross-curricular links
• Children to suggest ideas about why the plasticine man gets squashed	• Show a wheel – child to move it. How did it move? (it rolled) – similar activity in circle with a ball, block *slid* across a board, child opening a bottle of Coke/water, etc. to classify movement into swing, twist, roll, jump, hop, etc. (Use children to show hop/jump/swerve, etc.) • Use toy cars to demonstrate moving slowly/quickly. Compare speeds – bringing in vocabulary fast/slow/faster/slower – go further. • Make a model person using soft home-made dough – demonstrate how he becomes *squashed* if he is in a toy car which is rolled down a slope and *STOPPED*. Moving objects can hurt us if we stop them. Link to road safety. Group work • Children to make a soft model (for in a car) and show how he becomes squashed if stopped at bottom of a ramp. • Children to sort objects by criteria of how they move.	• Home-made play-dough Cross-curricular links Music – 'Wheels on the bus' song PE rolling, jumping, twisting, etc. Maths language – slow, slower, fast, faster, etc.
As for lesson A	B *Alternative lesson* (or perhaps additional children) • Visit to playground. Children to notice how swings/roundabouts, etc. move. • Return to classroom and draw pictures and annotate to show *how* they move, e.g. swing/slide/turn/spin, etc. • How do *they* move when they are on the rides? • What happens to 'dough man' when his car is moving fast down the real slide and then stopped? • Take two scooters. Can children scoot slowly and quickly?	• Parent helpers? • Letter to parents about the visit to playground • Dough man • Toy cars Cross-curricular links PSE • Walking to playground safely • Care and consideration for other playground users

Activity 2 *continued*

Science class 1E 4 lessons 1hr 30 mins each week		
Learning objectives	Learning experiences	Resources and cross-curricular links
Stage 3 Children should understand that pushes or pulls can make things speed up or slow down.	Watch video (*Think about Science – Push and Pull*) • Ask child to move a toy car or a box containing bricks. Has it been pushed or pulled? • Experiment with other articles – children to *move* them and identify *pushes* or *pulls*. *Tell* child that a *force* is a push or pull.	• Video – *Think about Science* – push and pull • Toy cars • Large box with toy bricks • String • Play-dough/flubber • Picture for labelling • Pictures for classifying
Vocabulary Move, push, pull, stretch, squash	• Can child make the toy car move by pulling? How could we do this? Children to think of a solution. • Show how a *big* push can make things move quickly, a *small* push slowly. • Show how a push against a moving ball can slow it down or stop it. Children in circle on carpet – 2 children demonstrate this. • Child to show how play-dough can be changed by pulling (use stretchy flubber to show this). Group work • Identify pushes and pulls on a picture (labelling) (HA) (MA). • Use storyboard to classify pushes and pulls. • Table with soft play-dough and flubber. Children to make shapes and change by pushing and pulling. • Children to go on forces safari and label with Post-it notes how doors/ cupboards, etc. are made to move (push or pull).	

Stage 4 Children should learn to:
• suggest a question to test
• predict what will happen
	• Children to explore with toy cars on ramps. Notice how they move. Describe movement.
	• Show how to change:
	  • height of ramp
	  • surface on ramp
		• Wood for ramps
		• Bricks – wooden or real
		• Box
		• Pull along toys
		• Push toys

Activity 2 continued

Science class 1E	4 lessons 1hr 30 mins each week	
Learning objectives	Learning experiences	Resources and cross-curricular links
• try it out • make measurements • discuss results	• different sorts of vehicles (types of tyres – e.g. home-made vehicle and wrap elastic bands onto wheels) • With children, decide on questions they might ask starting with 'What happens if . . . ?' • Children to devise own test (in groups) – guide if appropriate. • Discuss fair test and adapt. • Carry out test. Think about how to record the results. • Tell others about their investigations. • Group to use ICT to record results.	Cross-curricular links Maths – measuring either distance travelled or time taken for vehicles to move down ramp

Figure 4.2 Example of a trainee teacher's planning

Managing practical work with very young children

When you are planning the work for very young children between the ages of 3 and 5 it will usually be practical. Young children learn best by active involvement with materials. What the teacher has to do is to find a balance between work which the children can plan for themselves, using resources provided by the teacher and those which will need more teacher direction and interaction.

Activity 3

Here are some activities which the teacher of a class of 25 3 and 4 year olds has planned. It is expected that the work will take place over a period of two weeks (see Module 5). The outdoor area is partially covered and there is a grassy slope.

- investigating stretchy and non-stretchy materials – play-dough, flubber, elastic bands, foam rubber, wooden rulers, paper, plastic materials, fabrics, both stretchy and non-stretchy;
- water play involving containers with holes;
- sliding and rolling – wooden blocks, ice-cubes on a large tray, balls, cylinders, foam blocks in a variety of shapes, vehicles with wheels.

Activity 3 *continued*

Think about how this work might be managed. Some of it might be part of the continuous provision which teachers provide every day in classrooms where there are young children. Some might take place with the whole class and some may be planned for when children are working in small groups with an adult.

Complete the pro-forma in Figure 4.3 which might help you to structure your ideas.

Child-initiated enquiry Continuous provision	Focused task with an adult	Whole-class activity	Advantages and disadvantages of this type of organisation

Figure 4.3 Pro-forma for planning

Managing resources

If we are to help children to become independent and to design their own investigations, they will have to have access to a range of resources which will help them to carry out their enquiries. There will be equipment which is housed in individual classrooms and will be used frequently and there will be some more expensive or bulky items which have to be shared between classes. Children will be encouraged to decide what equipment they need in order to carry out a task and to collect and tidy away their own equipment. However, if they are to do this, then they will need easy access to the resources. Often very busy teachers take the easy option and choose to instruct the children how to carry out an investigation so that they can be sure that all resources are to hand and to prevent children wandering about the school in search of the elusive pieces of equipment. However, this will not help children to develop their own planning skills and will not help them to become independent.

It is frustrating for teachers who want their children to use force meters to find that they are being used by another class or that they have not been returned to a central store. If we are to manage the practical work effectively, then we need to have a suitable system for storing and collecting resources. The science subject leader is usually the person who is responsible for setting up an effective system and individual teachers are responsible for managing the resources which are stored in the classroom.

Activity 4

- How can the teacher encourage children to identify and collect their own equipment? How can this be encouraged with the younger children?
- List the resources for scientific enquiry which you think should be stored in individual classrooms. Consider how these would be stored to provide easy access. Describe a system for 'borrowing' from a central store.
- Choose one of the areas of science from the list below and suggest what pieces of equipment are (a) essential and (b) desirable in order to teach effectively and give the children the opportunity to pursue enquiry in small groups.

  - forces
  - investigating living things
  - light and shadows
  - sound
  - materials
  - earth and space

DISCUSSION AND REFLECTION

You will have been thinking about how to manage the practical work in science and about how to manage the lessons, and in doing this, you will have reflected on how the important aspects of good science teaching have to be incorporated into your planning and organisation.

In Activity 1 you will have watched a teacher at work and noticed how many of the aspects of good teaching were demonstrated. You will have reviewed the lesson and thought about whether or not the introduction was lively and stimulating and whether or not the work was linked to the children's everyday experiences and the teaching which had gone before. You will have considered the balance between practical work and whole class discussion and the way in which the teacher provided opportunities for children to express their own ideas. You will have thought about the timing of each part of the lesson and the way in which children were encouraged to become independent learners. You might have asked yourself whether they showed that they could plan for themselves and think about the question which they wanted to answer. There may be some people who would suggest that children should be told how to carry out the test so that they could have a clear focus on the science concepts which were identified in the learning objectives. Yet this will not help the children to develop their own planning skills. A skilful teacher will direct the children towards making the right decisions and help them to an understanding of how to collect results which can be analysed so that conclusions can be drawn. The more reflective teachers will also give children time to reflect on what they have learned and to evaluate the procedures which they have used. Perhaps you saw evidence of this in the video sequence which you watched.

In Activity 2 you will have thought about the key factors of good teaching which you identified in Activity 1. You will have discussed how to manage the lessons which are described briefly in the plan. Perhaps you might think that the general discussion about transport and the sorting activity should take place in a separate session from the investigations with autogyros. (These are the little paper spinners which are sometimes called paper helicopters.) Or you might think that the sorting could be going on while the teacher worked with other groups who were observing how the paper autogyros spun and fell to the ground. The teacher would want to draw the children's attention to specific factors such as the direction in which the paper spun while they were observing and it might be more profitable to do this in small groups so that questions such as 'What would happen if we shortened the wings?' could be thought about and perhaps tested at a later date.

You will have considered how you might introduce the activities and how you would arrange the classroom. You might even have suggested additional resources which you would use. The focus of your thinking will have been on how to group children, how long each section of the lesson should be and how you would enable all the children to complete enough practical work and notice enough detail so that they could express ideas about the science. Thinking and doing are both important factors in science learning. We can often forget the thinking if we get too enthusiastic about the doing but time for reflection is necessary. Harlen (2000) suggests that: 'This may mean less time for doing, but increased learning from what is done.'

In Activity 3 you will have noticed that similar resources are used for the experiences which you considered in Activity 2. The teacher has planned to use play-dough, and other materials which may stretch but, although the resources are similar, the approach to management will be completely different. There will be less emphasis on whole class discussion and more on providing situations where the children will learn through their play (see Module 5). There will be times when a focused task is planned for a small group. Occasionally the whole class may come together and sometimes the teacher provides resources for child-initiated play.

Child-initiated enquiry Continuous provision	Focused task with an adult	Whole-class activity	Advantages and disadvantages of this type of organisation
Flubber – exploring the properties of the material			Advantages: children have the time to explore on their own. Disadvantages: teachers are not always present to guide the enquiry and to develop vocabulary.
Play-dough – exploring, making shapes, cutting and making marks on the dough			As above
	Investigating a range of materials and sorting into those which can be stretched		Advantages: teachers can guide the enquiry and question children as appropriate. Disadvantages: all children might not have chance to take part.
Water play – having containers with holes available			Advantages: children have the time to explore on their own. Disadvantages: teachers are not always present to guide the enquiry and to develop vocabulary.

continued

Child-initiated enquiry Continuous provision	Focused task with an adult	Whole-class activity	Advantages and disadvantages of this type of organisation
		Introduction to the sliding and rolling activity. Teacher and children all together on carpet. Classify those objects which roll and those which slide down a slope. Discuss the terms sliding and rolling. Ask for children's ideas about why some objects slide and some roll. Think about the materials from which the objects are made as well as their shape.	Advantages: teacher has the opportunity to direct specific question at individuals. Teacher can guide the enquiry. Disadvantages: the management might be difficult with so many young children involved.
Follow-up activity to the whole-class exploration of sliding and rolling. Children to have objects available out of doors near to the grassy slope. Also to have a small ramp out of doors near to the objects so that comparisons can be made about the way in which the objects roll and slide down the two different slopes.			Advantages: children have the time to explore on their own. Disadvantages: teachers are not always present to guide the enquiry and to develop vocabulary.
	Ice cubes on a very large tray. Children to observe as the blocks slide across the tray. Draw out observations about the way in which the cubes slide as the tray becomes very wet.		

Figure 4.4 Examples of early years planning

You may have completed the pro-forma in a similar way to Figure 4.4, or yours may be completely different. There is no 'right' way to organise the activities but you might like to think about how appropriate the suggestions are. Do you think that it would be sensible to introduce the whole class to the sliding and rolling activity? They would be seated in a circle on the carpet. But might it get out of hand? Would this be better done as a small group task? As you evaluate the suggestions you will have tried to imagine that you are in the early years classroom and will have pictures in your mind of where the groups of children would be and the adult supervision which would be required.

In Activity 4 you will have been thinking about how to manage the resources which you need for practical science. Some resources are needed in every classroom and these will be those to which children need regular access. There are also the larger pieces such as model skeletons and microscopes which have to be shared. Some resources need to be purchased and others such as fabrics and pieces of wood can be collected by the children and teachers. If you are working with others, you will be able to share information about useful resources. Your

balances	string	polythene bags
timers	scissors	rubber bands
magnifiers	tape measures	measuring scoops or
funnels	play-dough	spoons
measuring cylinders and	plasticine	water containers
beakers	paper clips	bowls for mixing
yoghurt pots	paper towels	masses
for younger children	collection of seeds	magnifying collecting
balances	bubble blowers	boxes or containers
balloons	candles	jelly mould
balls	colour filters	cooking equipment
mirrors	cellophane	microscope
musical instruments	fabrics	mechanical toys
camera	cotton reels	wires
building blocks	batteries	cells
construction kits	fans	bulbs
garden tools	plastic pipettes	buzzers
plastic tubing	feathers	motors
straws	articles for the water tray	pooters
tuning forks	including water wheels and	bowls
wind gauge	watering cans	sand
woodworking tools	large paint brushes	rocks
prisms	food colouring	stethoscope
ramps	magnifiers	shells
wooden articles		sieves
plastic articles		squeezy bottles
aluminium foil		plastic syringes

Figure 4.5 Resources often kept in classrooms

school may have an equipment list which has been provided by your local education board or authority. There is also a useful book, *The Primary Equipment Handbook*, published by the Association for Science Education which gives advice on what could be purchased and collected.

Perhaps you might have suggested some of the following items bearing in mind the fact that the younger children need constant access to a very wide range of equipment.

The list in Figure 4.5 may not necessarily be identical to the one which you have produced but by consulting catalogues and sharing ideas with others you may have increased your knowledge of what is available and what is essential.

Children should learn to be independent and you will have thought about how the management of resources might help them towards this independence. If classroom resources are stored on open shelves which are clearly labelled, children will soon become used to collecting and tidying away items which they have used. Younger children are very capable of finding what they want if their resource boxes are identified with pictures.

Schools develop their own systems for the sharing of resources. Some schools have boxes into which they place the materials and equipment needed for each topic. Teachers then fill in a loan book and take the boxes to their classrooms. This system has drawbacks as many items of expensive equipment are needed for more than one topic. A more common approach is for a science storeroom to be set up with materials stored on open shelves. Teachers then remove items as they are needed and return them to the shelves. This system works as long as teachers are punctilious about returning items immediately they have finished with them. It is also useful to scrutinise long-term planning to make sure that resources can be allocated efficiently.

REFERENCES

Feasey, R. (1998) *The Primary Equipment Handbook*, Hatfield: Association for Science Education.

Harlen, W. (2000) *The Teaching of Science in Primary Schools*, London: David Fulton.

FURTHER READING

Coates, D., Jarvis, T., McKeon, F. and Vause, J. (1998) *Mentoring in Primary Science*, Leicester: SCIcentre, School of Education.

Collis, M. (1983) 'Resources for primary school science', in *The Teaching of Primary Science: Policy and Practice*, Sussex: Falmer Press.

De Boo, M. (2000) *Laying the Foundations in the Early Years*, Hatfield: Association for Science Education.

NCC (1993) *Teaching Science*, London: National Curriculum Council.

Module 5 · Science in the early years
– The foundation stage

INTRODUCTION

This module is concerned with planning the part of the curriculum that helps children to explore and understand the scientific aspects of their world. The activities focus on:

- identifying appropriate skills for the young children;
- learning through play;
- the adult role in supporting the learning.

In any discussion about the education of very young children aged between 3 and 5, most teachers will suggest that children need a secure and caring environment where they are given opportunities to play, explore, solve problems and investigate. When planning the curriculum, teachers make sure that children are actively and physically involved and that the contexts offer a framework for the development of competencies and understandings.

There has been a long tradition in early years education of identifying competencies which help children to become literate and numerate. There is also an emphasis on creative and physical development and in helping children to develop social skills. However, when considering the scientific process, many teachers are faced with a dilemma. They want to keep true to their philosophy about integrated, child-centred and child-initiated learning and at the same time help children to become scientific problem solvers. Hartley (2000) considers the value of problem solving and suggests that the process of trying to solve the problem develops thinking skills and is not just a means of finding a solution.

The teacher's role is crucial in this process. There will be times when the children and teachers investigate a problem together. There will also be times when the teacher responds quickly to identify a problem which the child has noticed but which to him seems insurmountable. For example, if the plasticine is hard when the child is trying to make a model, he or she may squeeze it a few times and then, finding it unsuitable, move away to play with something else. If the teacher identifies the problem quickly and poses a question such as, 'I wonder how we can make the plasticine soft again?', the teacher is acting as a role model for the first stage of the scientific process; the raising of a question to investigate. The problem is one to which the child can relate. The teacher may need to help the child think about how heat can soften the plasticine and will refer to previous experiences and build on the child's own knowledge of the warm places in the classroom and the sources of heat, in order to help the child to think about how to reach a solution.

There will be countless informal opportunities for this type of problem solving but there will also be times when the teacher will want to work with a group of children in a more structured way in order to think about the decisions which have to be made. Children should be encouraged to make decisions for themselves; for it is this question raising and decision-making which is at the heart of scientific enquiry. Activity 1 considers the skills of scientific enquiry and illustrates how very young children use these skills in contexts which are familiar to most nursery and kindergarten teachers.

When we are engaged in scientific enquiry we are not only developing skills but at the same time we learn about the materials which we are investigating; we learn science concepts. Activity 2 uses familiar contexts to consider a range of learning outcomes related to both concepts and skills. The skills under consideration are those which are generally accepted to be crucial to early development of thinking skills and communication:

- observation
- prediction
- problem solving
- decision-making
- communication.

At this stage of development children learn through interaction with materials, other children and adults in a play-based situation:

> Play is a fountain which brings children happiness and fun in their childhood. It is a creative activity allowing children to make decisions for themselves . . . adults should be partners and participants in play with children rather than the directors of the activity.
>
> (Ishiggaki and Lin, 1999)

Activities 3 and 4 consider the teacher's role in providing appropriate resources for both child-initiated and adult-initiated play. Teachers will provide areas which are set up for role play where children are free to act out their fantasies. If the materials are carefully chosen, there will be opportunities for children to learn science through their own explorations. Science will not be the only thing they learn when engaged in this type of play. It is impossible to separate the learning into 'subjects' at this early stage. The child who repeatedly pours water from one container to another will learn about the properties of this liquid. He or she will find the same liquid in his bath, when washing-up or helping to make a drink. He or she cannot fail to notice that it is wet, that it finds its own level in a container and that it comes down in the form of rain. At the same time he or she will learn about the capacity of the containers and will develop language skills in talking about what he or she is doing.

The two activities emphasise the difference between the two types of play and ask you to identify potential scientific learning.

In Activity 5 you will consider the role of the teacher when entering into dialogue with children. It is important for children to feel that they are taking part in a conversation in which their ideas and opinions are valued. The activity asks you to consider the options open to the teacher as he or she engages in play alongside the children. Sometimes the teacher will encourage observation through their own actions as when for instance blowing bubbles and showing delight. The teacher might say: 'Oh, look at the colours in my bubble! Has your bubble got the same colours?' Or he or she might, when playing in the sand, smooth out the sand and make marks with his or her finger before trying out other mark-making tools in the smooth sand. The dialogue with children is important, but it is useful for teachers to have a shared philosophy about how much they will say to children and when and how to interact.

Becoming scientific

When teachers in kindergartens and nurseries plan a developmental curriculum for science they first need to define the skills which they are hoping to develop. These skills cannot always be separated (Harlen, 2000, p. 31) but it is useful to think about each of them in order that appropriate experiences and resources can be provided. It is generally accepted that scientific enquiry involves the following:

- observing
- asking questions
- predicting
- planning investigations
- interpreting evidence
- hypothesising
- communicating findings.

These skills are used by scientists who might be 8 or 80 years old but are they used by 3 and 4 year olds and are they appropriate skills for these young children?

Activity 1

Read the vignette and consider the questions that follow.

Consider the following situation where a teacher is working with a small group of 4 year olds:

The teacher has a closed box by the side of her chair. She reaches into the box and pulls out a tin. She has made a tinfoil lid for the tin and secured it with an elastic band. She passes the tin around the group and asks the children to shake it. She asks if they think there is anything in the tin. There is no sound as the children shake the tin. Most children say that there is nothing in the tin. The teacher takes off the lid and shows the children that inside the tin is some cotton wool. She gets out another tin and again allows the children to shake it in turn. This time they do hear a sound as she has placed some marbles in the tin. She tries a few more tins which contain small pieces of wood, some plasticine and some sand. The children describe the sounds which they hear. They talk about soft sounds, tinny sounds, 'lumpy' sounds and swishy sounds. She then brings out a tin which is full of sand. The children can tell that the tin is heavy and they immediately say that there is something in the tin. However, they can hear no sound. One child suggests that there is no room for the 'stuff' to move.

The teacher presents the children with a collection of materials which include dried peas, sand, lentils, and the tops from old plastic pens. She also gives them a collection of containers with lids. The containers are tubular containers made of both metal and cardboard. She invites the children to make some shakers for themselves by putting the materials inside the containers. They play with these for a few minutes and talk about the sorts of sound which they hear. The teacher joins in the play. She then asks them to predict whether paper tissues, nails and a small plastic spoon would make a sound if they were put into the containers. They make their predictions and then test out their ideas. To finish off the activity she puts on a music tape and the children shake one of their chosen shakers in time to the music. She joins in with the play and shakes her own container. At group time later in the morning the children talk about what they have done and together they demonstrate their shakers in time to the music.

Have any of the skills of scientific enquiry been used by the children? Consider each of the skills in turn and note down any evidence which may indicate that children have been using the skills. The evidence may be indicated by children's dialogue or actions.

Encouraging thinking

Teachers of very young children provide an experiential curriculum and are often provided with guidelines which suggest that the children should be encouraged to develop the skills of:

- observation
- prediction

- problem solving
- decision-making
- communication.

While these skills may seem, at first glance, to be different from those skills which form the basis of scientific enquiry, if you examine closely what children actually do when they are learning science, you will find that many of the features of their thinking could be said to be developing the skills listed above.

Teachers are also anxious to develop independence in children and the ability to collaborate with other children and these too can be developed as children investigate the materials, plants and animals which make up their world.

Drummond (1995) reported on research which showed that, where activities made demands on children's powers to think for themselves and to solve problems, then the quality of the learning was high and the children were enthusiastic. Children can use their reasoning powers at a very early age and we have a responsibility as educators to provide opportunities for children to do this.

The recognition of opportunities for problem solving is usually done by the teacher at the planning stage, but, as children become more practised in thinking about problems identified by the teacher, they will perhaps move towards questioning for themselves. The solving of the problems is not always the main objective for the children; talking about the problem and trying out ways to solve the problem with adults are often seen as more important (Hartley, 2000). After children have worked with adults on exploration and problem solving over many months, they will perhaps be ready to move towards a more structured form of enquiry, where they begin to consider whether or not their tests are fair.

Activity 2

Use Figure 5.1 as a model and consider the anticipated skill development and concept development when providing one of the following learning contexts. Complete the pro-forma (Figure 5.2) to show how you would help children to develop skills, what the evidence of learning might be and the science concepts which could be developed. Do this in relation to the resource which you have chosen. You should handle some of the materials yourself before you consider the potential for learning. By exploring at your own level you will be able to consider what children might observe, what problems might be posed and what scientific concepts could be addressed:

- making and using cornflour slime (sometimes called Gloop or Ooblick);
- a plastic tank which has been converted into a temporary habitat for snails;
- white paint, red paint, black paint, flour, water, mixing palettes, spoons, brushes, straws and paper;

Activity 2 *continued*

- a collection of balls and skittles of various weights and sizes;
- a washing-up bowl containing soil and worms (be aware of Health and Safety Guidelines when including living creatures in activities);
- some peppermint essence or other strong smelling foods.

Resources and contexts
Soap flakes, bowls, water, variety of whisks.
Each child to have his own large bowl. After whisking the mixture until it is thick, it is tipped onto a plastic table so that children can handle it more easily.

	How to help children to develop the skills	Evidence of skill development	Science concepts which may be developed
Observation	Observe alongside the children. Show delight in certain features and point these out (e.g. dip hands in the mixture and then clap hands together)	Do children observe . . . ? • flakes floating before they are whisked; • that the more we whisk the more frothy the mixture becomes; • that the addition of more flakes changes the mixture; • the smell of the mixture.	Change in materials when they are added to water Change as air is whisked into the mixture Some small flakes float on top of the water
Prediction	Ask questions as appropriate to elicit a response.	Do children predict what will happen? When . . . ? • we add more flakes • we add more water • we squash the foam • we leave the foam for a long time • we sprinkle glitter dust onto the mixture	
Problem solving	Identify problems and encourage children to think about how to solve them, e.g. Can you make the mixture flat instead of frothy? Would washing-up liquid and water make the same sort of mixture if they are whisked together? Which is the best whisk for . . . ? Give children time to express their ideas.	Do children show by their words and actions that they are trying to solve the problems?	Change when air is squashed out of the mixture

Activity 2 *continued*

	How to help children to develop the skills	Evidence of skill development	Science concepts which may be developed
Decision-making		Do children choose own whisks? Do they talk about or show that they can test out the different mixtures and whisks? Do they decide how many flakes to add to the water?	
Communi-cation		Do children talk to the adult or other children as they work? Are they able to describe sequences of events to other children at group time? Are they able to sequence a series of photographs showing the stages of the activity?	

Figure 5.1 Whisking soap flakes: identifying and developing learning

Resources and contexts			
	How to help children to develop the skills	Evidence of skill development	Science concepts which may be developed
Observation			
Prediction			
Problem solving			
Decision-making			
Communication			

Figure 5.2 Pro-forma: identifying and developing learning

Learning through play

A curriculum for the early years will have been planned to include a wide variety of opportunities for play. However, it is not enough merely to provide the environment and resources. Practitioners will need to consider the learning outcomes and the needs of a particular group of children before they plan the environment. The needs of a child who has just turned 3 will probably not be the same as for a child who is almost 5. Some children in early years settings will be able to make decisions for themselves and to articulate ideas, while others will be at the stage where they play without speaking to other children and adults.

Some play is adult-initiated and some is child-initiated. A well-planned curriculum will include both types of play. Through interaction with materials and the exploration of these materials, children may learn scientific concepts and develop scientific skills. Curriculum developers often list these skills and concepts and suggest that practitioners plan to include opportunities for children to develop ideas and practise the skills. An examination of these guidelines shows that they might include:

- differentiating between hot and cold, wet and dry, rough and smooth;
- recognising some of the properties of materials and how they are used, e.g. waterproof materials, soft materials, transparent materials;
- realising that materials can change when, for instance, they are heated, stretched, mixed or whisked;
- recognising and identifying different materials;
- sorting materials;
- recognising and identifying some animals;
- realising that care should be shown to living things;
- knowing about the changes in the weather and the seasons;
- knowing when it is light and dark;
- knowing that some objects float;
- knowing how to move objects and begin to use the terms, push, pull, swing;
- knowing how we use our bodies to smell, taste, etc.;
- recognising and naming the main parts of the body;
- naming primary colours and knowing that mixing paints makes new colours;
- knowing about melting;
- knowing that some structures are stable and that sometimes high towers of bricks topple over;
- knowing that some objects roll and that some slide;
- suggesting ideas about why things happen;
- using magnifiers and tools correctly and safely.

This list is not exhaustive but the ideas will be familiar to early years practitioners.

The children will have the opportunity to learn some of the science ideas as they work and play alongside the teacher but some will be learned through an independent play situation. The classroom will be arranged so that children can develop ideas as they play in the various areas which have been set up by the teacher.

- There will be an area which is devoted to messy play and here you will probably find the sand and water trays, the painting easels and the mixing tables.
- There will be an outdoor area with large construction toys, a garden or some planters and perhaps climbing frames.
- There will be a quiet area with books, headphones and tapes.
- There will be a writing area with a variety of mark-making equipment.
- There may be a music area with instruments for the children to play.
- There will be a construction corner where children can build large models.
- There will also be tables with jigsaws, malleable materials and some living things.
- There will be a role play area where children can fantasise or be involved in social play.

Many teachers consider that in order for the children to practise skills and learn concepts there needs to be some stability in the location and types of resource which are provided. Children need to be able to repeat their play in order to test out ideas but, on the other hand, new materials and contexts need to be provided from time to time in order to enthuse and stimulate the children. There will therefore, in any early years setting, be a balance between newly introduced materials and those which are familiar to the children. As the seasons change, so will some of the living things in the classroom. Sometimes a new story will be introduced and this may stimulate a new topic for exploring. The role play area will change from time to time in order to introduce the children to new concepts. The outdoor area will be used to develop children's learning in all aspects of the early years curriculum.

Activity 3

Using the list of science ideas and the list of skills which you considered in Activity 1 identify the potential learning in one of the following role play contexts. Figure 5.3 provides an example of how you might do this:

- the garage and petrol station;
- the baby clinic;
- the hairdresser;
- the garden centre;
- the fire station (in outside play area);
- the hospital;
- the castle;

Activity 3 *continued*

- the shoe shop;
- the space station.

To be set up in covered area – linked to outside play area

collection of small brick
samples (available from local brickworks)
sand, water, trowels, mixing board

- *Large construction*
- *ramps and planks*
- *box of objects which slide/roll*
- *wheels from old bicycles*
- *construction kits with wheels, screwdrivers etc.*
- *set of large gears*
- *blocks*

The Workshop

pulley system
set up with a
small box attached
– small box and
articles for lifting

Shelves containing
articles to take
apart eg. old clocks

Workbench area *
- *small pieces of wood of different types*
- *sandpaper*
- *large nails*
- *short handled hammers*

* Always closely supervised

'Office' area with
telephone, paper and
mark-making materials.

Potential for learning

Science concepts	*Skills*
• *objects can be moved by pushing and pulling*	• *manipulative skills*
• *recognise and name gears – know that they link together and move together*	• *ability to select appropriate tools*
	• *collaboration*
• *some objects roll when pushed; some objects slide*	• *observing ways in which materials behave*
• *we can join materials with nuts and bolts and with nails*	• *noticing details of events which happen when they are handling materials*
• *structures need to be stable so that they don't topple over*	
• *some wood is easier to 'sand' than others*	

Figure 5.3 Outline planning: the workshop

Child-initiated and teacher-initiated play

The role play area is set up by the teacher and here children engage in both teacher-initiated and child-initiated play. The area is usually set up for a sustained period of time. Sometimes the teacher will want to put out resources on the carpet or on table tops. These are often provided for a shorter period of time so that a particular skill or concept can be developed. Figure 5.4 shows the roles required for teacher- and child-initiated play.

Child-initiated play	Teacher-initiated play
Teachers provide resources.	Teachers provide the resources.
Adults may join in the play but take the lead from the children.	The teachers take the lead in starting the play and suggest the context.
The teacher's role is to stimulate and encourage the play.	The teacher observes and monitors the learning.
The teacher observes and monitors the learning.	

Figure 5.4 Types of play

Consider the following scenario which illustrates teacher-initiated play:

The teacher wants the children to learn that some materials float and some do not and that sometimes the shape of the material affects this. He is not introducing the word sink at this time. He wants the children to play together and test out ideas.

In the water tray he has placed a sheet of aluminium foil which is floating on top of the water. He prods the foil and as it becomes covered in water it slowly sinks to the bottom of the tray. He then tells the children that he is going to make some boats. He shapes his foil into a boat shape and pushes it along the water.

'Oh, look!' he cries, 'It's floating.' He then crumples another identical piece of foil which sinks. He encourages the children to play with the foil and to try to make boat shapes. Some of the children are successful but many are unsuccessful. They do seem to be enjoying the experience and play quite happily, pushing the foil sheets under the water, lying them on top of the water and shaping some. After a few minutes the teacher introduces some foil cartons made of a thicker and firmer foil and he shapes one of these into a boat. He leaves the children at this point with the resources available nearby and suggests that the children might like to play by themselves for a while. He asks if they would like to try and make some boats.

Activity 4

Choose one of the following contexts and suggest how a teacher might plan to develop science skills and concepts through teacher-initiated play. Think about what the children might learn and how you would introduce the play:

- a table with magnets;
- the sand tray;
- the outdoor area with watering cans and water;
- a collection of toy vehicles.

Interactions with young children

In classrooms where very young children are learning, there are usually many adults. Some of the adults will be teachers, some will be trained assistants and some may be parent helpers. It is the teacher's role to plan for all the adults in the classroom. Generally, the curriculum planning is done by the whole team with the teacher taking responsibility for setting and monitoring the learning intentions. It is important that all the adults adopt the same approach when talking to the children, guiding their actions and playing alongside them.

In the photograph in Figure 5.5 you can see Stacey, who is 4 years old, washing the dishes after a cooking session. There is an opportunity here to talk

Figure 5.5 Stacey washing up

to the child about what she can see and feel. The temptation is to quiz and question her about the temperature of the water, the bubbles or what sponge or cloth is best for cleaning. Very often children do not respond to this approach. They need time to observe as well as the opportunity to think about their response when the teacher is talking to them. On the other hand, talk with children must not be minimal. We need our talk to be a genuine discourse which gives the child the opportunity to feel valued and confident and to engage in thought.

Activity 5

Would you intervene in this situation? If so, what would you say and do? Although questioning is an important part of teaching, it is not always appropriate to question children. Sometimes we can encourage learning, just as much by our actions, as by what we say.

In the photograph in Figure 5.6 you can see Callum looking at himself in a ripple mirror. What would you say and do?

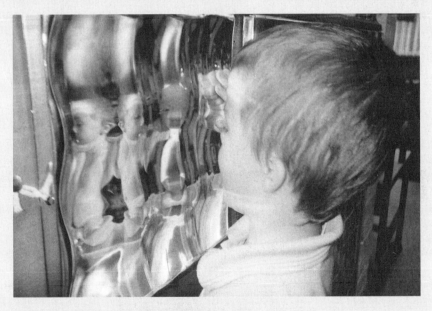

Figure 5.6 Callum looking in a ripple mirror

DISCUSSION AND REFLECTION

Activity 1

The scenario describes a focused task where the teacher is working with a small group of children. The teacher will have identified the anticipated learning outcomes at the planning stage. Your scrutiny of the text will have enabled you to consider what concepts and skills he or she was hoping to develop. It might be useful to consider each of these in turn.

Observation

You will probably have noted that the children are using their senses of sight and hearing to identify what is in the containers. It is not just a matter of noting whether or not a sound is made but of describing the sounds by using their past experiences. The teacher provides examples where no sound is made so that the children might begin to associate sound with the coming together of two materials. When they go on to make their own shakers they are using their earlier observations to help them to select appropriate materials. There are opportunities for the children to note similarities and differences, for example when they play with both metal cylindrical containers and those made of cardboard.

Asking questions

There are no examples here of children asking direct questions. However, it might be possible in situations like this for a child to indicate that there are 'questions in the mind'. As they choose the materials to put into their containers, they could well be wondering what sound would be made when they put on the lids and shake.

Prediction

You will have noted that the teacher asks the children to predict. The children will be basing their predictions, not only on past experiences, but also on the observations which they made. They could also be using their predicting skills as they select the materials for their own shakers.

Planning investigations

This involves making decisions about what to do in order to find an answer to a question or to test out an idea. In this particular scenario there are no examples of the children planning what to do. If children of this age carry out structured investigations they are usually guided by the teacher.

Interpreting evidence

The children can be seen to be interpreting evidence as they listen to the sounds which are made and suggesting what, if anything, is in the containers. They feel the tins and listen in order to suggest what might be in the tins and what type of sound is made.

Hypothesising

The child who says that, 'There is no room for the stuff to move', is not only interpreting evidence but is using his previous knowledge about the relationship with sound and movement to suggest an idea.

Communicating findings

Children were provided with the opportunity to do this when they described to their peers what they had been doing and what they had found out. The teacher's role is crucial in this process as he or she will have to prompt the children at an appropriate point in the discussion.

You will also probably have noticed that the teacher plays alongside the children and acts as a participating member of the group.

Activity 2

In this section you will have been considering how to develop the thinking skills which are at the heart of planning the curriculum for very young children. The contexts which are suggested will be very familiar to experienced teachers. By filling in the pro-forma you will have been able to focus your thoughts on how to help children develop skills and to consider the potential for skill and concept development.

When thinking how to help children you will have suggested problems which the children might consider. For instance when handling the paint and flour you will probably have suggested that children use straws to blow or drip splats onto paper and plastic surfaces. You will have helped children to notice how the paint soaks into the paper and stays in a 'puddle' on top of the plastic. If they move their plastic plate from side to side they will notice that the liquid flows. In order to encourage thinking, you will need to help children to focus on problems and to think about ways in which the problem can be solved.

If you asked, 'How can we stop the paint from moving on the plastic?', children might respond by suggesting that we make the paint thicker. If the children do not respond in the way in which you anticipate, then you will need to change your question to one with a tighter focus. For example 'Could we make the paint thicker by mixing something with it?' If the children still do not respond with suggestions, then you may even, eventually, have to mix some thick paint and some thin paint and ask the children to decide which moves least on the plate. As an extension to this, you could ask the children to paint a model which needs a 'thick' covering and ask them to mix their own paint.

Activity 3

This activity will have enabled you to consider the preparation of resources for a role play area and to identify the *potential* for learning. Although the children will use the resources independently, the consideration of how they might be used will have helped you to address some of the concepts and skills which are to be addressed in the early years. Teachers need to be creative and wide-ranging when considering this type of provision. For instance, when considering how to set up the garden centre, you might have considered the learning which could take place when children compared different types of seeds and bulbs, when they play in the potting trays or when they observe growing vegetables and flowering plants. You might also have considered the setting up of a garden centre café and even perhaps the making of simple plaster casts to represent garden ornaments. It is the close analysis of the provision which enables you to think about anticipated learning. You might also find it useful to consider the teacher's role when the children are playing.

Activity 4

The focus in this activity is on getting children started so that they can explore for themselves. This type of activity is different from a focused task where the teacher guides the children in a much more structured way. The potential for learning is identified but we cannot always be sure about the direction in which the children's play may go.

You will have your own ideas about the starting points for exploration and you may have had the opportunity to share ideas with colleagues. Perhaps some of the following starting points have been discussed.

Magnets

Placing a variety of materials in a sand tray and using a magnet on a string to find those which are attracted to the magnet or exploring with different sizes and types of magnet to see which part of the magnets attract objects made from iron and steel. Testing to see if magnets attract through paper, card, plastic, etc.

The sand tray

Have a tray of damp sand and a tray of dry sand. Play with a variety of moulds to encourage children to recognise the characteristics of the two types of sand.

The outdoor area with water and watering cans

Play with the watering cans and make patterns on the concrete playground. Use squeezy bottles to squirt water onto walls and other surfaces. Use brushes to 'paint' with the water.

A collection of toy vehicles

Push the vehicles on a variety of surfaces and slopes.

The starting points are not difficult to determine. However, if you are to observe children as they play and are to monitor the learning it will be helpful if you can establish the potential learning goals for the experiences.

Activity 5

The emphasis here is on deciding how to interact with the child. A well-chosen question might start off a dialogue in which the child feels a valued partner. Sometimes it is an observational comment which can begin a conversation. If for instance, when the child is looking into the ripple mirror, you say, 'Oh, look, I can see two of you. I can see the side of your head and the front of your head!', you will be focusing the child's observations. You could go on to move your fingers in front of the mirror and talk about what you notice. Later you might suggest that the child looks into a plane mirror which in many classrooms are hung next to ripple mirrors. Teachers should be aware of the opportunities for scientific learning in spontaneous situations such as these.

Science for young children is intrinsically embedded in exploratory play. The children are provided with resources to enable this learning to take place but the provision cannot be, and should not be, haphazard. It is the responsibility of all who are privileged to work with these very young people to make sure that good foundations and attitudes to learning are developed. Perhaps your reflections have enabled you to consider your own philosophy.

REFERENCES

Drummond, M.J. (1995) 'What are four year olds like? Setting the scene', in *Learning Properly? The Four Year Old in School*, Rochdale: OMEP.

Harlen, W. (2000) *The Teaching of Science in Primary Schools*, London: David Fulton Publishers.

FURTHER READING

De Boo, M. (ed.) (2000) *Laying the Foundations in the Early Years*, Association for Science Education

Desforges, C. (1993) *Children as Thinkers and as Learners*, London: British Association for Early Childhood Education.

Hartley, K. (2000) 'Encouraging problem solving', *Practical Pre-School*, vol. 23.

Hendy, L. (1995) 'Playing, role playing and dramatic activity', *Early Years*, vol. 15, no. 2, pp. 13–16.

Ishiggaki, E.H. and Lin, J. (1999) 'A comparative study of pre-school teachers' attitudes: towards "children's right to play" in Japan, China and Korea', *The International Journal of Early Childhood*, vol. 1, no. 31, pp. 40–7.

Module 6   Meaning and purposes of assessment

INTRODUCTION

There can be no doubt that the importance of assessment in education has grown enormously since the beginning of the 1990s. It is hard to believe that, in the 1980s, there was scarcely any assessment of science and virtually no records were kept in primary schools of children's progress in science. There are, of course, pros and cons to this change in the role of assessment. Since the prominence of assessment is not going to diminish, however, it is important for us to consider how to make use of it to improve children's learning and to make sure that any potential negative effects are minimised.

This module is one of five about assessment. It introduces general ideas and terminology and so is best read before other modules on assessment. Its aims are:

- to discuss the meaning, purposes and methods of assessment as applied to primary science;
- to consider the characteristics of, and relationship between, assessment for two purposes – to help on-going learning (formative) and to report on learning that has been achieved (summative).

There are four main parts, each involving an activity. The activity is best undertaken as part of a group. However, if this is not possible, then you should record your responses to the activities before reading the discussion at the end of the module, where some examples of others' responses are discussed.

The first part deals with the meaning and purposes of assessment. This could be rather dry and theoretical, but we go beyond the definition of terminology to look at what the words mean in action in the classroom. So Activity 1 takes a look at five events that could be part of any classroom practice and asks you to consider what was going on in relation to gathering and using information about children's learning. It brings in one of the most important distinctions to be made in assessment – about purposes. It is always essential to be clear about the purpose of an assessment, to take care that we do not use procedures appropriate for one purpose for a quite different purpose, and to make sure that the assessment is always used effectively to serve its purpose. Otherwise assessment can take time away from learning.

Although we list five aims on page 79, our focus is specifically on the first two: assessment to help learning (formative, or assessment *for* learning) and assessment to summarise learning achieved at a certain time (summative, or assessment *of* learning). For reasons given later, most attention is given in this module to formative assessment and the relationship between assessment for formative and summative aims.

In the second part of the module we look at the methods of gathering information for assessment and ways of interpreting it. This discussion will only make sense if, after the first part, you have a clear understanding that assessment involves *making a judgement* about the information collected. Often the judgement is automatic and therefore not obvious, for example, in a teacher's response to a child while in discussion of his or her work – but it is always there. This is because assessment replaces the actual evidence of learning; by a written or spoken comment, a mark, grade or 'level', etc.

We discuss three main ways in which we can make the judgement: by comparing a child's work with what the child has done before (child-referenced); by comparing it with a standard of performance that is the same for all children (criterion-referenced); or comparing with a norm or average expectation for similar children (norm-referenced).

Clearly, it is important to know how a judgement has been reached. A child-referenced comment may appear to value highly the work of a child who has made good progress even though the quality of the work may be quite low and would not in itself deserve such praise. When children are being compared with each other it would be unfair to use child-referenced judgements and a common standard or criterion has to be applied. Activity 2 asks you to look again at the five events discussed in Activity 1, focusing this time on the ways of collecting and judging the information about children's learning.

In the third part we turn to the characteristics of assessment for the two purposes we are looking at particularly – formative and summative. Summative assessment has been given a great deal of attention (and resources) in recent educational reforms, for example, in the development of national tests. Much less attention had been given to formative assessment. Recently this is beginning to change, however, as a result of uncovering firm evidence that improving the practice of formative assessment can raise standards of achievement. We refer to the review of research by Paul Black and Dylan Wiliam, *Inside the Black Box*, published in full in 1998, which distilled evidence from a large number of studies that all pointed to gains in learning as a result of changing practice of classroom assessment.

We also discuss other reasons for valuing formative assessment, relating to the approach to learning which takes seriously pupils' own ideas and uses them as a starting point. Formative assessment begins by finding out where children are in their ideas and skills and therefore is part of this approach to teaching and learning. But this is not all. As we will see in later modules, it is important that the information gained about the children's understanding is used in deciding what are the appropriate next steps in learning and helping children to take them. Involvement of the pupils in this process means that they, the ones who do the learning, know what they are trying to do. So sharing goals of learning with pupils and helping them to assess their own progress are part of what is needed. Hence the aspects of formative assessment are embedded in teaching and are part of it, not an added extra. With these points in mind, Activity 3 asks you to make explicit your ideas about the nature of assessment for formative and summative purposes and the major difference between them.

We need both formative and summative assessment because they serve different purposes. But it is necessary to have a balance between the two. In current practice it seems that summative assessment too often takes precedence and dominates teaching and learning – to the point of 'teaching to the test' in some classrooms and certainly taking time to practise test taking. So, in Activity 4, you are invited to consider the relationship between the two and the action that might enable both purposes of assessment to be met without compromising the value of either.

THE ACTIVITIES

Read the following five vignettes, A to E. Then, for each one, answer the questions in Activity 1.

A

The overarching topic was 'materials' and the teacher of 9 and 10 year olds was embarking on a section about changes in materials. The goal of this section of the work was to enable children to recognise the origin of some materials in everyday use and the ways they have changed to reach their familiar form. She planned to assign groups a different common material (such as silk, cotton, wool, linen, paper) or food (milk, sugar, flour, chocolate) to explore by first-hand investigation and find out further information using books and other sources. They would then share their findings with the whole class.

Before setting up the group work, however, the teacher decided to find out the initial ideas of the children about one of these materials and at the same time show them a way in which they could report their work. She showed them a silk scarf and asked them to produce four sequenced drawings of what the scarf was like before it was a scarf, what it was like before that, and again before that, and before that (as suggested in *Nuffield Primary Science* Materials). They worked in pairs and had a piece of paper for their drawings, as shown in Figure 6.1.

Materials	What it was like before that	and before that	and before that	and before that
The scarf				

Figure 6.1 Pro-forma: production of the scarf

The children discussed their ideas and worked on their drawings in pairs for about 30 minutes and then the teacher asked them to pin their drawings on a large board she had prepared for this purpose. Once done, the children looked at each other's drawings and had plenty of questions to ask in the ensuing class discussion.

The collage of drawings gave the teacher an immediate overview of the children's way of tackling this work as well as of their ideas about the origin and changes in this particular material. She noticed that most recognised that the material had been woven from a thread and had been dyed before or after weaving, but few had an idea of the origin of the thread from a living thing, a silk worm. All the materials that she had chosen for them to study originated as living plants, so she was alerted to paying attention to this first link in the chain of changes. She also noted that their drawings were not self-explanatory and so she discussed with them how they could make their drawings clearer. She showed some examples of drawings with labels that helped anyone looking at them to understand what was being represented. The children were then put to work in groups of four, each group being given a different material on which to work.

B

In a different class the children were investigating the dissolving of sugar in water. Some groups were trying different kinds of sugar – icing, granulated, castor, brown, coffee crystals – and some were seeing what difference stirring made to the rate of dissolving. One group was working on the effect of temperature on how quickly the sugar would dissolve. They had some ice cold water, some water at room temperature and some warmer water from the hot tap. They were careful to take the same quantity of the same kind of sugar and to add it in the same way to each sample of water and to stir them all the same amount. However, the teacher noted that they were using different volumes of water. As they were clearly aware of keeping things the same for fair comparison, the teacher asked them if they thought it mattered that there were different volumes of water. They said it wouldn't make any difference, because the sugar would dissolve whatever the amount of water. The teacher realised that this had implications for their understanding of what is going on when a substance dissolves in water. So he asked them to try a separate investigation – of taking a small volume of tap water and adding a large amount of salt. When they found some would not dissolve, even with vigorous stirring, they added more water until it did all dissolve. Without using the word 'saturated' they talked about a certain amount of water only being able to hold a certain amount of salt, so the more water, the more salt would be able to dissolve. They then went back to their sugar investigation realising that the volume of water was likely to be a variable they had to control for a fair test.

C

At the end of their investigations of dissolving, the teacher held a discussion with the whole class about what they would need to know about each group's work in order to understand what had been done, what had been found and how it could be explained. They ended up with a list of points that made a good report of an investigation. The teacher wrote these in large print on a chart and pinned them on the wall. While the children wrote their reports of their investigation they were reminded to pay attention to the points listed. When they presented their reports to each other, they used the list to make constructive comments about how the reports (their own and those of others) could be improved.

D

In another class, at the end of the unit on materials the children were given some questions to answer in their notebooks. Here are some of them:

1   What will happen when these things are put in water? Tick 'float' or 'sink' for each one:

	Float	Sink
Metal bottle cap upside down		
Cork		
Apple		
Bottle full of water		
Small coin (5p)		
Large coin (50p)		

Figure 6.2 Questions on floating and sinking

2   Describe what you would do to find out which of three different kinds of paper towel soaks up most water.

....

....

3   How can these mixtures of materials be separated? Tick the methods that would work for each one.

Mixture of	Use a magnet	Add water and then filter	Use a sieve
Sand and salt			
Cement and gravel			
Sand and iron filings			

Figure 6.3 Pro-forma: separation of materials

E

At the end of each year a school gave a standardised test of study skills to every pupil so that pupils in each class could be compared with the norm for their age group and their progress from year to year could be monitored.

Activity 1

For each of the events described in vignettes A, B, C, D and E, decide whether in your view it involves assessment. If so, identify what information was gathered, by whom, about whom, how it was used and what was the purpose of the assessment, and complete Figure 6.4.

	A	B	C	D	E
Was there assessment?					
What information was gathered?					
By whom was it gathered, about whom?					
Who used it and how?					
What was the purpose?					

Figure 6.4 Assessment features

The meanings of assessment

Gathering information about children's ideas and skills in an informal way, as in vignettes A and B, is part of teaching and it is equally part of assessment. The term 'assessment' is used to include a wide range of methods by which information is gathered and appraised. Assessment is more than description; it always involves:

- collecting evidence in a planned and systematic way;
- interpreting the evidence to produce a judgement;
- communicating and using the judgement.

Assessment can be initiated and conducted by those inside the classroom – teacher and pupils – or those outside, as in externally devised tests and examinations or visiting researchers.

Purposes

Assessment can serve a range of purposes:

- to help children's learning (formative assessment);
- to summarise achievement at certain times (summative assessment);
- to evaluate the effectiveness of teaching (where the focus of interest is the class not the individual);
- to monitor the performance of children across a locality, region or country (where only a sample of students is assessed);
- to assist in research or evaluation of curriculum materials.

Our concern here is with teachers and children in primary classrooms where the main purposes of assessment are the first two of these. That is:

- to find out where children are in their learning in order to identify the next steps that are appropriate (formative assessment, or assessment *for* learning);
- to find out what children have achieved at certain points in order to monitor progress and to report this to parents, other teachers and the children themselves (summative assessment, or assessment *of* learning).

Everything about assessment – the methods used to gather information, how judgements are made, what use is made of the judgements – should serve the purpose of the assessment. So it is very important to be clear about the purpose when any assessment is planned or undertaken. Indeed, the difference between formative and summative lies not in how the assessment is carried out (for the same methods can be used to gather information for either purpose) but in the use that is made of the information.

Assessment procedures

Information about children's achievements can be collected by:

- questioning in ways that elicit their understanding and skills;
- observing them carrying out their regular class work (observing includes listening, questioning and discussing);
- studying the products of their regular work (including drawings, artefacts, writing);
- introducing special activities into regular class work (e.g. concept mapping, diagnostic tasks);
- giving tests (teacher-made and external; performance and written).

These are methods of collecting evidence, they should *not* be described as *methods of assessment*, for the reason that assessment also involves *making a judgement*. How this judgement is made is an important aspect of an assessment.

Making a judgement means that the information is compared with some expectation, standard or criterion, which can be done in three main ways:

- Sometimes the expectation is specific to a particular child, as when a teacher gives an encouraging response or sign (which can be just a comment or smile) to a child's work because it indicates progress for that child. (This is child-referenced assessment, sometimes described as ipsative.)
- Sometimes the expectation is based on what is normal for children of the same age. (This is norm-referenced assessment.)
- Sometimes the expectation is expressed in terms of certain levels of understanding or skill. (This is criterion-referenced assessment.)

Activity 2

For each of the events A to E identify the main methods of gathering information and the basis used in making judgements about the children's achievements, then complete Figure 6.5.

Event	Method used to gather information	Basis of making a judgement
A		
B		
C		
D		
E		

Figure 6.5 Judgement of children's achievements

Formative and summative assessment

The assessment in vignettes A, B and C falls into the 'formative' category, while vignettes D and E describe summative assessment. Think of an example of formative assessment and one of summative assessment and describe it to your group as you begin Activity 3.

Activity 3

Bearing in mind various examples of formative and of summative assessment, identify the defining characteristics of assessment for each of these purposes. Think about, for instance:

- how the assessment relates to learning;
- who is involved, in what ways;
- when it takes place;
- what special conditions are needed if any;
- what it leads to.

Then write a list of bullet points to describe formative assessment and another to describe summative assessment.

The importance of formative assessment

In this and the other modules on assessment we are paying most attention to formative assessment, although we also refer to assessment for summative purposes. The reason for this emphasis is the recognition of the considerable potential for raising children's achievement by improving practice of formative assessment.

The two most important reasons for focusing on formative assessment are:

1 It is essential to learning and teaching which starts from children's existing ideas and skills. Arguments for this approach are explored in Module 3. When teachers want to take into account the ideas and skills that children bring to a new situation, it is clearly important for them to find out what these are. Only by doing this can these starting points be taken into account and new learning be based on firm foundations. If teachers do not do this, there is a danger of requiring children to take steps that are too large for them, so that they can only follow blindly, without understanding. If the steps are too small, then children are not challenged to develop their ideas and opportunities for learning are missed. But it is not just at the start of new experiences that such information is needed. As ideas and skills develop, there is a continuing need to see how children are conducting their enquiries and making sense of new experiences. Thus

gathering information – and importantly using it – need to become part of teaching.

2   There is evidence from research that practising formative assessment is a significant element in raising achievement, especially that of lower achieving children. A review of research in this area (Black and Wiliam, 1998) found that introducing certain practices characteristic of formative assessment had the effect of improving learning to a greater extent than any other intervention. The characteristics of classroom practice associated with these gains in learning are that:

(a)   assessment is used by teachers to adapt teaching;
(b)   teachers give feedback to children in terms of how to improve their work, not in terms of judgemental comments, grades or marks;
(c)   children are actively engaged in learning – meaning that they are active in developing their understanding, not passively receiving information;
(d)   children are engaged in self-assessment and in helping to decide their next steps;
(e)   teachers regard all children as being capable of learning.

Balancing formative and summative assessment

Summative assessment is needed for reporting what children have achieved, but it does not change that achievement. As the term suggests, it gives a summary of achievement, not a detailed account as is necessary to help learning. This summary can be the result of reviewing a child's work over the relevant period, or the result of giving a test, or a combination of both of these. Often the summary is expressed as achievement at a particular level, or meeting a certain standard or achieving a score in a test. Sometimes – indeed, all too often – the meaning behind the levels, standards or scores is forgotten and achieving the label becomes an end in itself. When this happens, summative assessment tends to dominate teaching and learning and formative assessment is submerged.

Summative assessment is even more likely to come to dominate teaching when the results for a whole class or school are used to evaluate a teacher or the school. This practice is controversial, but widespread. When information from assessment is used in this way, and particularly if it is made public, the assessment has important implications for the status and reputation of the teacher or school (it becomes 'high stakes'). The more that depends on the assessment, the more attention is given to ensuring that the results are as far as possible unbiased. And because there is a widespread assumption that tests are more reliable than teachers' judgements (despite lack of real evidence to support this claim), the desire to make things 'fair' leads to a preference for tests rather than using teachers' judgements to summarise achievement. Now the most reliable tests are the ones that focus narrowly on knowledge that can be assessed as 'correct' or 'incorrect', so the more reliable the test, the less information they can give about skills and concepts that are not so easily tested. When the results are important to teachers, they understandably focus on those things that children need to know to succeed, and so end up teaching children to pass tests rather than helping them to achieve the full range of goals of science education.

Activity 4

Consider the points made about formative assessment and summative assessment:

- In your experience, is there a conflict in practice between formative assessment and summative assessment (or assessment for learning and assessment of learning)?
- What do you think can be done to ensure that assessment can serve formative and summative purposes, without the needs of the latter dominating the former?
- In your view, can assessments for these different purposes be combined or should they be kept strictly separate?

DISCUSSION AND REFLECTION

Activity 1

In event A the teacher set out to find out the ideas of all the children in the class and planned a neat way of doing this so that she, and all the children, were able to see the range of ideas and the understanding of origins and changes in materials that were held. This put her in a position of providing experiences that would challenge those children whose ideas were incomplete, were based on everyday thinking, or just uninformed. So she had gathered information to use in adapting her teaching. She may or may not be able to use the information about the particular views of individual children; most probably she would arrange activities that enabled children to test their ideas, by investigation and using information sources, and thus allow for individual differences. The assessment was thus formative in planning for the whole class.

In event B, the assessment is less obvious. What the teacher is doing seems a normal part of interaction with groups of children. Because of this, some people do not identify the event as involving assessment. However, the teacher was gathering information about the children's use of enquiry skills and realising that they needed help. In contrast to event A, the teacher was focusing on individual children and took immediate action. Although we often discuss the gathering of information and the use made of it as separate steps, in formative assessment they generally occur together and the teacher uses the same situation in which the information was gathered to take action, as in this case. The assessment was formative for the individual children involved rather than for the class as a whole, as in A.

In event C the teacher was helping children to assess their own work. In order to do this they needed to know what were the criteria by which to judge it. Had the teacher just given them a list of 'what makes a good report' (which she could easily have done) there would be a risk that the children would not understand the meaning and would apply the criteria somewhat mechanistically. By asking them to decide 'what makes a good report', the teacher ensured that the children were using criteria they understood, were considered appropriate to them and to which they had committed themselves. Thus the children themselves would be judging their work and in doing this deciding what they had to improve. The assessment was thus formative in improving their work through self-assessment.

In event D there was obvious assessment using questions devised by the teacher. Since these were given at the end of the unit, however, the results could not have a formative role in the learning relating to the unit. The same information was gathered about all the children. We can speculate that the teacher

	A	B	C	D	E
Was there assessment?	Yes	Yes	Yes	Yes	Yes
What information was gathered?	Ideas about origin and changes in materials; representation of these changes	Ideas about factors influencing dissolving	Criteria for judging quality of chn's reports	Ideas about properties of materials and planning investigations	Score on study skills test
By whom was it gathered, about or from whom?	Teacher about all chn in the class	Teacher about individual chn	Teacher from class	Teacher about all chn in the class	Teacher about all chn in the class
Who used it and how?	Teacher in next teaching step	Teacher in adapting learning activities of individuals	Children in self- and peer assessment	Not known (presumed to add to record of chn's achievement)	Not known (presumed to add to record of chn's achievement)
What was the purpose?	To adapt teaching of whole class to chn's ideas and skills (formative)	To help individual chn's learning (formative)	For chn to be self-assessing during on-going work (formative)	To check on what chn had learned in the unit (summative)	To compare chn with average for their age (summative)

Figure 6.6 Assessment features

might use this in reflecting on his or her teaching for the next time he or she taught this unit with another class, or aspects of what was or was not under- stood might be used in a general way in adapting teaching. Otherwise it is not clear how the information could be used in a formative manner. The purpose is more obviously summative, so that the overall progress of the children could be recorded.

In event E the purpose is quite clearly, and almost only, summative. Although it is always possible to look at the errors in tests made by individual children and use this diagnostically, such information is better gained in other ways. A score on a norm-referenced (standardised) test indicates an overall judgement of how a child compares with others, and does not give details of what it is they are succeeding in doing and where they need help. The purpose here, then, is probably, as in event D, to create a record of achievement. This discussion would lead to the pro-forma being completed as shown in Figure 6.6.

Activity 2

The above discussion has covered most of the points relating to the method of gathering information. In making the judgement involved in the assessment, the teacher in event A would be using criteria concerning the particular understanding about materials appropriate to the stage of the pupils. Thus this is criterion-referenced assessment, the same criterion being used for all the pupils. In event B, however, the teacher was judging what individual pupils were doing in relation to what he expected them to be able to do. Although he would have the general aim for all the pupils in mind, the immediate judgement would be child-referenced. Event C produced criteria, developed by the pupils, that were used by all, so that their self-assessment was criterion-referenced. (The argument that it is child-referenced because the children devised the criteria could be countered by pointing out that there were

Event	Method used to gather information	Basis of making a judgement
A	Studying products of work	Criteria based on understanding and skill (same for all)
B	Observing regular class work	Child-referenced criteria (ipsative)
C	Discussing regular work	Criteria developed by consensus (same for all)
D	Teacher devised tests	Criteria based on understanding and skills (same for all)
E	Standardised test	Norms for age group (norm-referenced)

Figure 6.7 Criteria for judgement

no individual criteria, which is the chief feature of child-referenced judgement.) The summative assessment in events D and E used different bases for judgement, criterion and norm-referenced respectively. These points would lead to the table being completed as shown in Figure 6.7.

Activity 3

Here is an example of formative assessment (quoted in Harlen, 2000):

> Julie's group had been collecting seeds of many different kinds. Julie added a sticky bud with the scales removed to the collection. She told the teacher that the things inside were seeds. When the teacher asked her what she thought was surrounding the little 'seeds' she said they were leaves that would grow into horse-chestnut leaves. She was convinced, however, that the things inside were the seeds of the tree. The teacher recalled the 'conkers' that they had collected some months earlier and how some of them had sprouted. But although Julie seemed to appreciate that conkers would grow into trees, they did not seem to fall into her idea of seeds. The teacher asked Julie how she would be able to collect the 'seeds' that she had identified. She said they would show when the sticky buds opened. So more twigs were gathered and Julie and other children observed the buds regularly as they opened. Later they continued observation of the opening of buds on the tree from which the twigs had been taken and noted that the 'seeds' turned into flowers and the new small conkers began to form. These various activities extended Julie's idea of the life cycle of plants as well as her notion of the variety of forms that seeds can take. At the same time all the children learned that trees had flowers, which they had not recognised before.

The aim of this work was to help the children to develop understanding of the cycle of changes in living things, in this case, in plants. The teacher hoped that the children would see that the bud already had the beginnings of flower inside it. She finds Julie with different ideas and takes them seriously and tries to understand what has made her connect the inside of the buds with seeds. She attempted to get Julie to rethink this idea by referring to the large horse chestnut seeds (conkers) that they had collected some months before, but that did not make her change her mind. So the teacher decided to let Julie test her idea by seeing if her prediction was correct. We can interpret this as the teacher deciding that the way to help Julie's learning was to let her obtain some evidence in relation to her idea, not to tell her that it was wrong. Although the step of observing the opening of the buds was not planned initially, it became part of the activity and the assessment of Julie's needs informed this next step. There was no comparison of Julie with any other pupil, just as assessment in relation to her own progress towards the goal of the lesson.

This illustrates some of these characteristics of formative assessment:

- It is part of teaching – an on-going and regular part of the teacher's role.
- It helps teachers – and pupils – to decide the appropriate next steps.
- The information about pupils' learning is judged against individual progress towards the goals of learning.
- Pupils are not compared with each other.

If we were to analyse other situations, as in events B and C, for example, we could add the following points:

- It can provide information about all kinds of learning outcomes – skills, concepts and attitudes.
- It can be conducted in all learning contexts.
- It involves pupils in self-assessment and helps them to decide their next steps.

An example of summative assessment

At the end of a topic on camouflage, which had been concerned with its use by soldiers in World War One, and which had involved a considerable amount on investigation of the visibility of various colours and patterns against different backgrounds, the teacher asked the children to write down their answers to these questions:

Why do we find white bears in the Arctic and brown bears in Canada?

What could be the reasons for fish being a pale colour underneath and a darker pattern on their backs?

The teacher marked the written answers, giving a mark out of 10 and a comment about how well the learning from the camouflage investigation had been used in the answers. She recorded the scores in her mark book. The papers were returned to the children the following week, when they had moved on to another topic.

The assessment here took place at the end of the work on camouflage and was not used to inform the progress of that work. It served to provide a record of the achievement of the children at the end of the topic. All the children were given the same questions to answer and their answers were all judged in the same way, using some criteria relating to application of ideas. In this case, the criteria used were not made explicit. This assessment has features which are characteristic of summative assessment, that is:

- It is carried out at certain times when a summary of achievements is required.

- It involves judging pupils' achievement against the same criteria or norms.
- It enables comparisons to be made among children, if required.
- It requires special conditions so that judgements are 'fair'.
- It indicates what children have achieved.

Activity 4

Some comments made by teachers which may reflect some of your own thoughts about the questions in Activity 4 are shown below:

> There is not necessarily a conflict – I can see that you need to do both, but is there time for all this assessment? If I have to choose, I do the summative because I have to do this – the school procedures demand it – and in any case I know what to do – I'm not so sure about what to do for formative assessment.

> I can see that formative assessment is important, but if I do it properly I need to spend so much time with individual children – this just isn't possible with thirty-two in the class.

> I think we do too much summative assessment and it's discouraging for some children. I make sure that they get rewarded for effort and not just the level of achievement.

> To stop summative assessment dominating? Well, just do less. We actually do more than is required because we think that practising the tests will improve achievement – it improves test scores but not learning. We should put learning first and have faith that the test scores will improve without letting them dominate what we do.

> I get the kids to assess themselves; that is automatically formative because they know what they've done. My job is to help them do it effectively. They collect their work and are very critical when they look back over it. They see what progress they've made, which is encouraging.

> Using a portfolio approach, I can assess formatively as we go along as far as the products of their work is concerned, then I summarise at the end of term and there's no need for a test.

> Formative assessment is quite different from summative assessment. It needs different kinds of information, at different times. I don't see how the two can be combined.

Perhaps like some of these teachers you are unsure of what formative assessment means in practice, or you feel locked into a routine of regular testing, or you don't have time to deal with individual children's learning however much you would like to.

What next?

Depending on your own views and concerns you might like to follow up one or more of the aspects of assessment considered in other modules:

- Module 7 deals with the practical matters of how to gather information during learning so that it can be used to help children take their next steps. It deals with the development of enquiry skills, which are so important in science yet so difficult to assess. The principles can be applied to the development of attitudes.
- Module 8 deals with assessing children's ideas and conceptual understanding.
- Module 9 emphasises the importance of helping children to understand the goals of their work and thus to be in a position to be able to assess their own progress and to use this insight in deciding how to make progress. When children are routinely self-assessing, the teacher is able to spend more time with individuals or small groups, in the knowledge that the others will be making decisions about working towards their goals.
- Module 10 concerns another key factor in formative assessment, the way in which teachers feed back their judgements on children's learning. Emphasis is placed on looking carefully at children's work and being sure about the evidence relevant to the goals of learning. Feedback to the child should then indicate ways forward if the assessment is to be formative.

REFERENCES

Black, P. and Wiliam, D. (1998) *Inside the Black Box*, London: School of Education, King's College, London.

Harlen, W. (2000) *Teaching, Learning and Assessing Science 5–12*, 3rd edn, London: Paul Chapman Publishing.

Nuffield Primary Science (1995) *11 Teachers' Guides and 22 Pupils' Books for Key Stage 2*, London: Collins Educational.

FURTHER READING

Assessment Reform Group (2002) *Assessment for Learning: Ten Principles for Guiding Classroom Practice*. See the ARG website: www.assessment-reform-group.org.uk

Module 7   Assessing enquiry skills

INTRODUCTION

This module is about assessing the development of children's enquiry skills. It involves realising that these skills do develop and recognising the signs of development in what children do. We are accustomed to thinking of concepts as being developmental, with children's early ideas being limited by their experience and gradually extending to encompass a wide range of events or objects, that is, becoming 'bigger'. So, for instance, children's ideas of what is an animal will begin by including only furry mammals and then extend to other animals with legs, then to include such things as worms and fish, and eventually take in all living things sharing certain characteristics. It is the same with enquiry skills; they develop from less to more mature forms as children's experience of enquiry grows. Having some idea of the general direction that this development takes is an essential key to helping this area of learning. If we have in mind a sequence of development and if this is expressed in ways that mean we can recognise development from how children go about their work, then we can recognise the children's level of attainment, and identify the next steps to be taken.

Children are using enquiry skills whenever they are gathering evidence and using it to develop their understanding. Enquiry does not always involve practical (hands-on) work, it can be conducted using 'second-hand' evidence, in the form of information from books, CD-ROMs, the Internet or other, including human, sources. Indeed, topics such as ones relating to the Earth and space have to rely on such evidence. We recognise that 'thinking' is as important as 'doing' in learning science and that children can test their own and others' ideas by using evidence that they could not themselves collect directly. However, there is no doubt that direct manipulation of material and objects is important for primary children because they tend to think in concrete rather than abstract terms, and whenever possible we use the real thing (or models of it, as in the case of the solar system). So enquiry skills of all kinds have a central part to play in learning science.

In order to help children develop their enquiry skills we need to know what they are presently able to do, just as to help the development of scientific ideas we need to know what their existing ideas are. But, unlike ideas, children do not describe and explain their skills, rather, they show in their actions what they can do. As a consequence, this means two things:

- knowing what to look out for as indications of the use of certain skills;
- knowing how to interpret observations in terms of development.

So the first of the four activities in this module is an exercise in thinking about the sequence of behaviours that indicates development of enquiry skills. Activity 1 provides sets of statements relating to these six enquiry skills: questioning; predicting; planning; gathering evidence by observing and measuring; interpreting evidence and drawing conclusions; communicating and reflecting critically. The statements describe different points in development of the skills, but are presented in random order. The task is to try to arrange them so that they describe a developmental sequence as closely as possible.

It helps to have the statements on cards or pieces of paper so that they can be shuffled physically. If you can do this activity with a group of other teachers who are familiar with different age groups, the inputs from their various experiences are particularly helpful. Other statements can be added to fill any gaps in development or in the kinds of behaviour that are included for each skill. You may not want to tackle all six skills at once, although it is necessary to have them in sequence for Activity 4. (You will find that two have been done for you in Figure 7.1.)

Activity 2 is a simulated trial of the use of the developmental criteria in assessing practical work. In the workshop situation the participants take different roles, as 'investigators' or 'observers'. One pair of observers uses the developmental criteria and the other a more open form for describing observations relating to specified skills. An alternative activity is to use the observation schedules in other situations, observing a group of pupils engaged in a practical investigation. Use only the lists for one or at most two skills at first. Any activity will serve for this purpose, the lists of skills being selected as appropriate to the focus of the investigation (e.g. include planning if it involves a fair test and observing if it is looking at similarities and differences). If the age group is suitable, you could set a group of children the task suggested in Activity 2 and try using both kinds of observation instrument yourself. If you have older children, it would be interesting, too, to share the developmental criteria with them (just for two skills) and ask them to assess themselves.

The purpose of Activity 3 is to apply the developmental criteria to children's written work. A point to be emphasised here is the need to look very carefully at the work. In a group workshop situation it is helpful to insist on two minutes for everyone to study a piece of work and then to describe what they see. It is quite striking how different people notice different things; pooling their observations enables everyone to 'see' more in the work. So when working alone, try to spend two minutes on each of the three pieces of work given here; put them aside and return to them again later and you will probably see something you overlooked before.

Having decided what is the evidence in each piece of work, try to match it with the developmental criteria. You will not, of course, be able to form any definite conclusion about the point of development each child has reached. It requires several different pieces of evidence from each child including observations of practical activity. However, as an exercise, we can take what we have and ask the question 'What would be the next steps for these children?' This is a vital stage in using assessment formatively, to help learning. Hopefully you will see how the statements, when arranged in developmental order, help to answer this question. What is important in formative assessment is using the information to help development; it is not necessary to label the work as being at a particular level.

In Activity 4 we turn briefly to summative assessment and consider the use of developmental indicators when the purpose of the assessment *is* to summarise learning in terms of the level reached. Of course criteria at progressive levels already exist in the form of the National Curriculum or the 5–14 Guidelines in Scotland or the Northern Ireland Curriculum, etc. But if we can relate the developmental criteria to these national levels, then the information already gathered for formative assessment can be used for summative assessment without collecting extra information or trying to use tests, which are inherently unsuitable for assessing the enquiry skills of individuals. So Activity 4 provides opportunity to see how the developmental indicators relate to the national levels and consider the pros and cons of using them in summative assessment.

INDICATORS OF ENQUIRY SKILLS

The following are lists of possible indicators of six main enquiry skills: questioning; predicting; planning; gathering evidence by observing and measuring; interpreting evidence and drawing conclusions; communicating and reflecting critically.

The statements in the lists are presented in random order. Choose one of these lists initially for Activity 1, then repeat for other lists if there is time.

Raising questions

1 Recognising a difference between an investigable question and one which cannot be answered by investigation.
2 Helping to turn their own questions into a form that can be tested.
3 Asking a variety of questions.
4 Suggesting how answers to various questions (investigable and non-investigable) can be found.
5 Participating effectively in discussing how their questions can be answered.

6 Recognising that only certain questions can be answered by scientific investigation.

Predicting

1 Using past experience or knowledge to make a prediction.
2 Justifying a prediction in terms of relevant science concepts.
3 Explaining the reason for a prediction in terms of patterns in available evidence.
4 Making a reasonable prediction based on an explicit hypothesis (possible explanation of what is going on).
5 Attempting to make a prediction relating to a problem or question even if it is based on pre-conceived ideas.
6 Recognising that a prediction is different from a guess.

Planning

1 Succeeding in planning a fair test using the support of a framework of questions.
2 Identifying what to look for or measure to obtain a result in an investigation.
3 Suggesting a useful approach to answering a question or testing a prediction by investigation, even if details are lacking or need further thought.
4 Identifying the variable that has to be changed and the things which should be kept the same for a fair test.
5 Selecting and using equipment and measuring devices suited to the task in hand.
6 Spontaneously structuring a plan so that variables are identified and steps taken to make results as accurate as possible.

Gathering evidence by observing and measuring

1 Taking steps to ensure that the results obtained are as accurate as they can reasonably be and repeating observations where necessary.
2 Succeeding in identifying obvious differences and similarities between objects and materials.
3 Identifying points of similarity between objects where differences are more obvious than similarities.
4 Taking an adequate series of observations to answer the question or test the prediction under investigation.
5 Using their senses appropriately and extending the range of sight using a hand lens or microscope as necessary.
6 Distinguishing from many observations those which are relevant to the problem in hand and explaining the reason.

Interpreting evidence and drawing conclusions

1 Recognising that there may be more than one explanation which fits the evidence.
2 Identifying patterns or trends in their observations or measurements.
3 Drawing conclusions which summarise and are consistent with all the evidence that has been collected.
4 Using patterns to draw conclusions and attempting to explain them in terms of scientific concepts.
5 Recognising that any conclusions are tentative and may have to be changed in the light of new evidence.
6 Discussing what they find in relation to their initial question or comparing their findings with their earlier predictions/expectations.

Communicating and reflecting critically

1 Comparing their procedures after the event with what was planned in order to make suggestions for improving their way of investigating.
2 Regularly and spontaneously using printed and electronic information sources to check or supplement their own findings.
3 Using tables, graphs and charts when these are suggested to record and organise results.
4 Choosing a form for recording or presenting results which is both considered and justified in relation to the type of information and the audience.
5 Using appropriate scientific language in reporting and showing understanding of the terms used.
6 Talking freely about their activities and the ideas they have, with or without making a written record.

Activity 1

Read the statements of indicators of pupil actions relating to six enquiry skills. The indicators are in random order. For one set of statements initially:

- Decide if you think there are others to add or if some are not relevant.
- Consider whether you think there is a developmental sequence within the statements for a particular skill, that is, that you would expect children to do what is described in some of the indicators before others.
- Try to arrange the indicators in order of development from early stages to later stages.
- Discuss the extent to which the sequence would be generally applicable and, if not, what might influence the extent to which children use certain skills.

It helps to have the statements written on card or separate slips of paper.

These indicators are criteria for use in assessment. They are described as 'developmental' when the statements are arranged as closely as possible, but still necessarily roughly, in terms of the development of the skills.

Having the development of skills in mind enables teachers to do the following:

- know what to look for in gathering information about enquiry skills by observation;
- interpret children's actions in terms of their development of enquiry skills;
- identify the next steps that are appropriate for the further development of the children's enquiry skills.

They can also be used for summative assessment, as we will see in Activity 4. In both cases, however, it is necessary to conduct observations on several occasions, since the content of an investigation limits the skills that can be observed and may also influence a particular child's performance (for instance, if the subject matter is familiar or not). This has to be remembered while undertaking Activities 2 and 3 since we can only deal with one example and have to assume that it is typical across a range of activities.

Activity 2

If possible, work in groups of six and give each member a specific role:

- two will be investigators who will undertake an investigation (I);
- two will be observers (X) using the lists of indicators of enquiry skills, rearranged as developmental criteria;
- two will be observers (Y) making notes on what is done in relation to these same sets of enquiry skills.

It is possible to work with only one observer in each group, as long as there is more than one investigator.

Part 1

Investigators (I)

Using the equipment provided (and any other you need) work as a pair to investigate the following:

- What happens to the water level in a container when a large piece of plasticine is totally immersed in the water, and then when the plasticine is made into a shape so that it floats on the water? Do you think there will be any difference in what happens to the water level in these two cases? Will it depend on the shape of the floating plasticine?
- Discuss and write down your predictions before you start.

Activity 2 *continued*

- Then find out what happens.
- Try to explain what you find.

Observers (X)

Using two of the lists of developmental criteria decide from what you observe which of the statements apply to the skills that they show. Just observe, do not interact with the investigators.

Do this in any way that you find works. You may find the pro-forma (X) in Figure 7.1 of help (the statements for two of the most relevant sets of skills are listed in developmental order as identified by other teachers).

Gathering evidence by observing and measuring	
Do the investigators:	
(a) succeed in identifying obvious differences and similarities between objects and materials?	
(b) identify points of similarity between objects where differences are more obvious than similarities?	
(c) use their senses appropriately and extend the range of sight using a hand lens or microscope as necessary?	
(d) make an adequate series of observations to answer the question or test the prediction being investigated?	
(e) take steps to ensure that the results obtained are as accurate as they can reasonably be and repeat observations?	
(f) distinguish from many observations those which are relevant to the problem in hand and explain the reason?	
Interpreting evidence and drawing conclusions	
Do the investigators:	
(a) discuss what they find in relation to their initial questions or compare their findings with their earlier predictions/expectations?	
(b) identify patterns or trends in their observations or measurements?	
(c) draw conclusions which summarise and are consistent with all the evidence that has been collected?	
(d) use patterns to draw conclusions and attempt to explain them in terms of scientific concepts?	
(e) recognise that there may be more than one explanation which fits the evidence?	
(f) recognise that any conclusions are tentative and may have to be changed in the light of new evidence?	

Figure 7.1 Pro-forma for observers (X)

Activity 2 *continued*

Observers (Y)

Using the pro-forma (Y) in Figure 7.2, make notes of your observations about how the investigators are using the same two sets of skills ('gathering evidence' and 'interpreting evidence'). Just observe, do not interact with the investigators.

Gathering evidence by observing and measuring	
Interpreting evidence and drawing conclusions	

Figure 7.2 Pro-forma for observers (Y)

Part 2

When the investigation has been completed (after about 20 minutes) spend the next 10 minutes as follows.

Activity 2 *continued*

Investigators

Use the pro-forma for Observers (X) to assess your own performance in relation to the two sets of skills.

Observers (X) and (Y)

Compare your observations among all the observers, focusing on the ease or difficulty of using the method assigned to you.

Finally, discuss as a whole group of six, the different experiences of self-assessment and observing with and without using the lists of indicators. Focus not so much on the performance of the investigators as on the process of assessment and particularly the role of the indicators.

Not all evidence of enquiry skill development takes the form of actions. What children say, write and draw can also provide evidence. This can add usefully to what is observed, particularly because it can be studied after the event, but it is important always to have evidence from what children actually do and not just what they say they have done. Moreover, as you will see, the written work can only give very limited evidence in relation to enquiry skills.

Activity 3

Consider the three pieces of work at the end of this module (Figures 7.5, 7.6 and 7.7). What can you find that is evidence of the six process sets of skills considered here? Where would you place the children in terms of the developmental criteria?

How would this judgement help you in deciding the next steps for these children in relation to developing enquiry skills?

Using developmental criteria in summative assessment of enquiry skills

Summative assessment, as its name suggests, provides a summary of what has been achieved at a certain time. The observations of actions and study of products made over an extended time can be reviewed against the developmental criteria and used for summative assessment. The summary often takes the form of saying that a child has reached a certain level of performance. Of course a great deal of information is lost in doing this and, most importantly, the answer does not indicate what to do to help learning. But that is not the purpose of summative assessment. This is why it is essential to be clear about the purpose of assessment. Levels are useful in summarising achievement, but they do not improve achievement.

In order to arrive at a summative assessment of enquiry skills we do not need to give a test or make further observations of children's written work. Indeed, the nature of enquiry skills means that to do this would produce a very unreliable judgement. This is because the use of enquiry skills depends a good deal on the content of the enquiry. So we should collect observations across a range of content as part of teaching and combine the findings in making a judgement about the level achieved (using the levels 1 to 8 of the National Curriculum or A to F of the Scottish 5–14 National Guidelines, or other national or local curriculum statements). Activity 4 explores how this process compares with the developmental criteria we have been using.

Activity 4

(a) For this you will need a copy of the level criteria that apply to the curriculum of your school. Consider the developmental criteria for 'raising questions', 'predicting', 'planning investigations', 'gathering evidence by observing', 'interpreting evidence and drawing conclusions' and 'communicating and reflecting critically' in relation to statements in the curriculum at the different levels.

   Does the result confirm your judgement about the sequence of development, in Activity 1?

(b) On the assumption that the work of the children considered in Activity 3 is typical of their work during the period for which achievement is being summarised, what level does this suggest they were working at?

(c) Discuss the pros and cons for different purposes of using the more detailed description of skill development in the six sets of criteria compared with the direct use of the curriculum level statements.

DISCUSSION AND REFLECTION

Activity 1

While you are trying to put the statements in order of development, using your experience of children, it may come into your mind that the sequence is not always the same. Sometimes a child can do something that indicates quite an advanced level of skills and at other times may not be able to do something relatively simple. In other words 'it all depends'. Whether or not a skill can be applied in a particular situation does indeed depend on what content the skill is to be used on. For instance, a child might well be able to 'Identify the variable that has to be changed and the things that should be kept the same for a fair test' if the content is familiar (something like 'which ball bounces highest?') but not if it is unfamiliar ('which solution has the highest osmotic pressure?').

Things children do that are indicators of raising questions	Things children do that are indicators of predicting
1. Ask a variety of questions 2. Participate effectively in discussing how their questions can be answered 3. Recognise a difference between an investigable question and one which cannot be answered by investigation 4. Suggest how answers to various questions (investigable and non-investigable) can be found 5. Help to turn their own questions into a form that can be tested 6. Recognise that only certain questions can be answered by scientific investigation	1. Attempt to make a prediction relating to a problem or question even if it is based on pre-conceived ideas 2. Recognise that a prediction is different from a guess 3. Make a reasonable prediction based on an explicit hypothesis (possible explanation of what is going on) 4. Explain the reason for a prediction in terms of patterns in available evidence 5. Use past experience or knowledge to make a prediction 6. Justify a prediction in terms of relevant science concepts
Things children do that are indicators of planning investigations	Things children do that are indicators of communicating and reflecting
1. Suggest a useful approach to answering a question or testing a prediction by investigation, even if details are lacking or need further thought 2. Identify the variable that has to be changed and the things which should be kept the same for a fair test 3. Identify what to look for or measure to obtain a result in an investigation 4. Select equipment and measuring devices suited to the task in hand 5. Succeed in planning a fair test using the support of a framework of questions 6. Spontaneously structure a plan so that variables are identified and steps taken to make results as accurate as possible	1. Talk freely about their activities and the ideas they have, with or without making a written record 2. Listen to others' ideas and look at their results 3. Use drawings, writing, models, paintings to present their ideas and findings 4. Use tables, graphs and charts when these are suggested to record and organise results 5. Use appropriate scientific language in reporting and show understanding of the terms used 6. Compare their actual procedures after the event with what was planned and make suggestions for improving their ways of investigating

Figure 7.3 Indicators of enquiry skills

Because of this interdependence of process and content, some people consider that enquiry skills do not develop but that children just become able to use them more widely as they become older and learn more content. However, research that has been carried out to look at skills using content familiar to children shows that there is indeed a development and that the older and more experienced the children are, the more they are able to pose investigable questions, to plan scientific investigations and to interpret what they find.

It still remains that a child might be capable of using a skill at a certain level but might not do so if the content seems uninteresting or difficult. This has implications for assessment. We should not judge from one situation but gather information in a range of activities, especially where the child is fully engaged with the content.

You might like to compare your sequences with those shown in Figure 7.3 that other teachers have produced.

Activity 2

When you tried them for the first time, you probably found it quite difficult to use the developmental indicators. They really have to be 'in your head' rather than 'in your hand' to be most useful. This happens over time. However, after you have tried using the indicators in observing children, you will have recognised the value of having attention directed at significant aspects of what the children do rather than trying to observe everything.

What teachers have found in comparing observation using the list of indicators with the open description is that they like a combination of the two. So having a space for comments beside the indicators is a useful way of providing for this. Those who use the free description during the observation often find that they missed information that others noted. This is sometimes because they have been busy writing but sometimes they didn't 'see' something even though they were looking at it, that is, they were not alerted to noticing it.

Remember that observations have to be made in a variety of circumstances and activities which give opportunity for pupils to show what they can do. The main value of the indicator lists is to ensure that evidence will be picked up and gradually accumulated to show where the children have reached in development of the skills.

If you did share some of the indicators with pupils, you might ask them to say which of the things listed they thought they did or did not do and how they judged this. Self-assessment of this kind involves a capacity to reflect on their own learning and it is interesting to see how far they are able to do this. For more on self-assessment, see Module 10.

Activity 3

As noted at the start of this module, it is important to look carefully at what is actually there in the children's work. For instance, in James' 'melting ice' investigation in Figure 7.6, is there really the evidence of the conclusion that 'the hotter it is the quicker the ice melts'? No temperatures were taken and there is no mention of what happened to the one in the sun. Probably we don't expect a 6 year old to measure temperatures, but we might expect him to use his results to answer the initial question more directly.

As part of formative assessment the criteria can be used as an aid in deciding the next steps in learning. The teacher would gather information either by observing or looking at a range of work with the criteria in mind and then review what has been found for each child in terms of the statements. In a typical situation there would be evidence of skills meeting the first few statements, then a point would be reached where there is uncertainty followed by statements higher in the list where there was no evidence of achievement. The point of uncertainty indicates where the child has reached and where he or she can be helped to make further progress. There are various ways of helping development of skills discussed in Module 4. For the moment we keep the focus on gathering information about achievement and turn briefly to the relationship between formative and summative assessment.

Activity 4

It is not easy to find exact parallels between the statements in the lists of indicators and the National Curriculum levels. Indeed, exact matches would not be expected because the aims of the two sets of statements are different. The indicators have to be more detailed if they are to serve a formative purpose and

Gathering evidence by observing and measuring	National Curriculum level	5–14 Guidelines level
Identifying obvious differences and similarities between objects and materials	1	
Identifying points of similarity between objects where differences are more obvious than similarities		
Using their senses appropriately and extending the range of sight using a hand lens or microscope as necessary	3	C
Making an adequate series of observations to answer the question or test the prediction being investigated	4	D
Taking steps to ensure that the results obtained are as accurate as they can reasonably be and repeating observations	5	D
Distinguishing from many observations those which are relevant to the problem in hand and explaining the reason	6	

Figure 7.4 Developmental criteria

so it can be expected that some indicators will not be reflected in the national documents which have to be more general. Do not spend too long on trying to find a match, just enough to decide whether the same kind of progression in skills is present in the curriculum as in the sequence that you identified in Activity 1.

An example of how one set of the indicators seems to be matched in curriculum documents is shown in Figure 7.4.

In other lists there are more 'gaps', for example, prediction is only mentioned at levels 4 and 5 on the National Curriculum and at level B and C of the 5–14 Guidelines. At the same time, this exercise might highlight gaps in the developmental criteria either within the six skills or the need to add to them. You could develop additional lists or modify the six we have discussed here to reflect your experience of skill development.

In part (b) of the activity remember that we have very little information to go on and therefore cannot expect to determine the levels of working of the

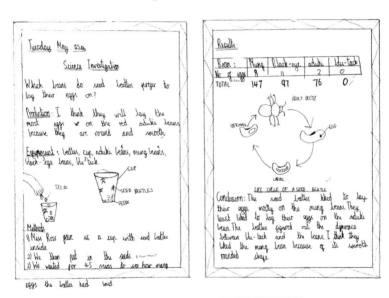

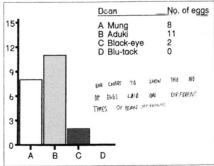

Figure 7.5 Children's drawing 1

AN INVESTIGATION

1] What am I trying to find out ?

I wanted to find out that if all the Ice cubes melt at the same time but in different places.

2] What do I need ?

I need a tray of Ice cubes. They have to be the same because its not fair to have little ones and big ones.

3] What did I do ?

①I put one in the sun ②I put one in the class. ③I put one outside ④one in my hands ⑤one in the freezer. ⑥one in the fridge. ⑦one on a heater

4] What happened ?

·The one in the hand and on the heater melted quikest. The one in the fridge was the slowest. the one in the freezer won't melt.

5] What have I learnt ?

·The hotter it is the quicker it melts.
·The colder it is the slower it melts.

Figure 7.6 Children's drawing 2

pupils who produced the work. It is more important to consider the possibility of using the information gathered for formative assessment for summative assessment.

Clearly there would be advantages in using information gathered for formative assessment for summative assessment also. There are particular advantages in doing this for the assessment of enquiry skills because the information is derived from a range of activities and thus is more valid than information derived from a test or single investigation. The practical problems are in keeping records so that the information gathered and used for formative assessment can be summarised in terms of national criteria. Hence the importance of seeing some parallels between the statements used as indicators for formative assessment and the National Curriculum level statements.

Finally, it is most important to emphasise that *while formative assessment information can be summarised to give summative assessment information, this cannot be done in reverse*, that is, summative information is too general to be used to guide specific decisions about how to make progress.

Upper Junior Science Investigation planning sheet and graph.

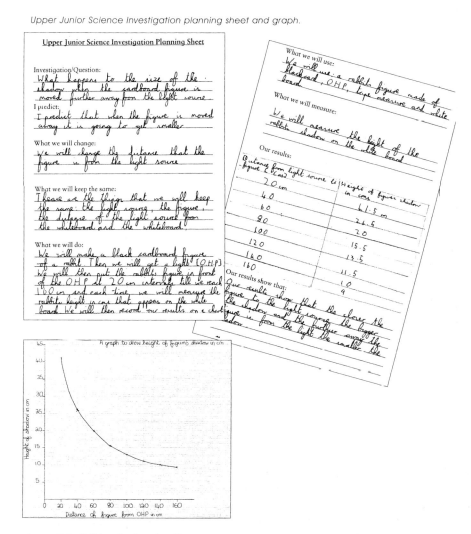

Figure 7.7 Children's drawing 3

REFERENCES

Harlen, W. (2000a) *The Teaching of Primary Science*, 3rd edn, London: David Fulton Publishing.
Harlen, W. (2000b) *Teaching, Learning and Assessing Primary Science*, 3rd edn, London: Paul Chapman Publishing.

FURTHER READING

Assessment Reform Group (2002) *Assessment for Learning: Ten Principles for Guiding Classroom Practice*, Cambridge: Assessment Reform Group.
Black, P. and Wiliam, D. (1998) *Inside the Black Box: Raising Standards through Classroom Assessment*, London: School of Education, King's College, London.

Module 8   Assessing children's conceptual understanding

INTRODUCTION

In this module we look at the assessment of children's understanding of science concepts in the context of using that information to help their progress. In some ways, this module complements Module 7, in that it deals with the notion of progression in an important outcome of learning. However, unlike enquiry skills which can be developed (and assessed) in all activities regardless of the topic, concepts are closely related to the topic studied. Thus we have to consider a number of different ideas and progression within each one. However, even within a topic, such as 'sound', whether ideas about hearing come before or after ideas about sources of sound depends entirely on which the children experience first. So we have to find a more satisfactory way of defining progression in understanding. This means thinking about overall changes in the nature of concepts that indicate progression.

    Using the word 'understanding' means that we are concerned with the way in which children make sense of their experience. Understanding is not something that we have or do not have, for phenomena can be understood at different levels. Take the concept of 'dissolving', for example. Young children can understand this in terms of a solid 'disappearing' in a liquid, although still being there in some form. Later it will be more broadly conceived in terms of gases going into liquids and liquids into liquids as well as solids into liquids. In secondary science dissolving may be 'understood' in terms of the molecules of one substance being distributed among those of another. At a much more advanced level the graduate chemist would think in terms of the electric charges of groups of atoms that cause some to be brought together and others to be kept apart. Thus there is indeed a progression in the understanding of this concept – although we do not expect children to go as far as the graduate chemist. So, clearly, understanding grows with experience and, in the process, the ideas or concepts become 'bigger', meaning that they link together and help to explain a larger number of phenomena. 'Small' ideas explain only a particular event, or ones closely related to each other. Young children are satisfied with small ideas until their experience extends and then they have to link related ideas together to make more widely applicable ones.

Another way of looking at this is to suggest that the small ideas that young children accumulate are the building blocks of later understanding. If they remain as single bricks, however, they do not constitute later understanding any more than a pile of bricks constitutes a house.

These issues are addressed in Activity 1, where two sets of ideas about living things are presented in random order. In attempting to arrange them in a sequence of development it is necessary to decide what, if any, features suggest that some are appropriate to early stages of development and others to later stages. If you find it difficult to decide which of two ideas is prior to the other, think why this may be. Perhaps you think the ideas are too specifically related to the subject matter and so dependent on which is taught first. It may be that, even if you cannot put all the ideas into a single sequence, you can make broad distinctions between two groups – for earlier and later development. Think about the basis on which you make a sequence or grouping of the ideas.

The other activities in this module concern ways of gathering information about children's ideas. In contrast with assessing enquiry skills, written work and drawings are a major source of information. Since it is only possible to assess certain ideas when children are working on relevant topics – you cannot assess ideas about circuits when they are sorting autumn leaves – it is important to be able to gather information about all the children's ideas at one time. So it is convenient to be able to use evidence on paper, which can be studied after the event, rather than the more ephemeral evidence from children's actions needed for enquiry skills. Activity 2 looks at work gathered in the normal course of classroom activities. The children were set certain tasks, but the point of this activity is to identify the ideas the children have rather than to decide whether they were successful in doing what the teacher asked.

One of the points emerging from Activity 2 is the importance of setting the task for writing and drawing in such a way that the children will communicate their ideas, that is, say what they are thinking, or explain what they observe rather than just describing it or drawing it. Concept maps are a particular form of drawing that requires children to express their ideas about how things relate to each other. These are introduced in Activity 3.

Concept maps are schematic ways of representing relationship among concepts. If we take the two concepts 'green' and 'leaf' we can relate them to each other in terms of the relationship that we understand links them, as shown in Figure 8.1.

The arrow indicates the direction of the relationship and the words written beside it form a proposition about how the two are related. That is, 'leaves may be green', but not 'green may be leaves'. We can add to this by linking to other words, so forming a map of inter-related concepts.

Concept maps have become widely used in primary classes and a number of variations and adaptations have been made by teachers. Some of these can be

Figure 8.1 Concept map

followed up in various articles in *Primary Science Review* (see Further Reading). Activity 4 presents some examples of children's concept maps and opportunities to consider how information from them can be used in formative assessment, to help decide the next steps in learning, and summatively to decide whether children have achieved certain levels of attainment.

Activity 1

Understanding of ideas shows in pupils' ability to apply them rather than just recite them. Here are some ideas about living things – one set relating to the processes of life and the other to the interaction of living things and their environment. They are presented in random order. For each set:

(a)   Consider whether there is a developmental sequence within each set of ideas, that is, would you expect children to be able to understand, and apply, some before others?
(b)   Try to arrange the ideas in order from early stages of development to later stages.
(c)   Discuss the extent to which the sequences indicate broad differences between ideas placed towards the beginning and the end of the sequences.

Ideas about the processes of life

(a)   There are organs within the bodies of mammals arranged in systems which carry out the major life processes.
(b)   Living things produce their own kind.
(c)   There are different kinds of living things called plants and different kinds called animals, which include human beings.
(d)   Animals and plants depend on each other in various ways.
(e)   All living things are made of cells.
(f)   Human beings need certain conditions to promote good health and body maintenance.
(g)   The basic life processes are common to plants and animals.

Ideas about the interaction of living things and their environment

(a)   The remains of living things will, in most circumstances, decay and this process releases substances that can be used as nutrients by other organisms.

(b)   Changes occur in living things in response to daily and seasonal changes in the environment.

(c)   Human activity can interfere in the balance between resources and the plants and animals depending on them.

(d)   Competition for life-supporting resources determines which living things survive and in which location.

(e)   Human activities can produce changes in the Earth's surface and atmosphere that can have long-term effects.

(f)   Plants are the ultimate source of food for all living things.

(g)   Different plants and animals are able to live and find food in very different places.

Activity 2

How much can you tell about children's understanding of scientific concepts from their written work?

(a)   Look at the pieces of work that follow and decide which of the ideas, listed in (i), (ii) and (iii), they give some information about.

(b)   In order to decide the extent to which the child has grasped an idea, you no doubt want to have more information. So suggest, in each case, what the teacher might do to find the extra information.

(i) Ideas about sound

What does this tell us about the child's understanding	Figure 8.5	Figure 8.6	Figure 8.7
Of how to produce sound			
Of the difference between pitch and loudness			
Of how the sound produced by an instrument can be changed			
About sound being produced when objects vibrate			
Of how to change the pitch and loudness of the sounds produced by musical instruments			
That sound travels through solids, water and air			
Of how the pitch of a sound made by a particular instrument can be raised or lowered			

Figure 8.2 Pro-forma: child's understanding of sound

Activity 2 *continued*

What the teacher needs to do to get more information:

....

....

(ii) Ideas about light

What does this tell us about the child's understanding	Figure 8.8	Figure 8.9	Figure 8.10
Of light being essential for seeing things			
That there are many sources of light			
That the Sun is the source of light for the Earth			
That shiny objects are not light sources and need a light source if they are to shine			
That we see objects when light from them goes into our eyes			
That light is reflected off objects			
That the position, shape and size of a shadow depend on the position of the object and the light source.			

Figure 8.3 Pro-forma: child's understanding of light

What the teacher needs to do to get more information:

....

....

Activity 2 continued

(iii) Materials

What does this tell us about the child's understanding	Figure 8.11	Figure 8.12	Figure 8.13
That there is a great variety of materials			
Some materials are natural and some are made by chemical processes			
The uses of materials can be related to their properties			
Materials can be changed into different forms			
Some materials can be changed permanently by heating and changes in other materials can be reversed by cooling			

Figure 8.4 Pro-forma: child's understanding of materials

What the teacher needs to do to get more information:

....

....

Activity 3

(a)   Working alone, draw a concept map which shows your ideas about how these things are connected. Make sure that you show a direction on the linking lines and label them to indicate the relationship.

Hot	Candle	Metal
Cold	Oven	Wood
Temperature	Fire	Plastic
Air	Draught	Insulation
Thermometer	Burn	Heat

(b)   When you have finished, exchange maps with a partner and compare your ideas. You should ask for explanations of links that you do not understand and be prepared to justify the links in your own map.

Activity 4

Concept maps can be used to reveal children's initial ideas before an activity, to identify changes in ideas after an activity compared with beforehand, and to assess a child's level of understanding. Refer to the maps in Figures 8.14 to 8.18 for the various parts of this activity.

(a)   The maps in Figures 8.14 and 8.15 were drawn by top infants at the start of activities on growing seeds. What can be found about the children's initial ideas? How might the teacher use this information in planning the focus of the work?

(b)   In Figures 8.16, 8.17 and 8.18 compare the 'before activities' maps with the 'after activities' maps. The activities the children were involved in between these times were

- using a thermometer to measure the temperature of a variety of things in the classroom;
- heating food (chocolate, bread, eggs) and observing the effect;
- discussing winter clothing to keep them warm;
- using their hands to assess temperature.

Identify the nature of the changes in terms of, for example, integrating new information into their ideas, creating more relationships, changing previous misunderstandings. List the changes for each one.

(c)   To assess the level of understanding, some basis for comparison is needed. One such basis is a map showing the links that you consider would be appropriate for a child of that age and experience. To try this, compare the map you drew in Activity 3 with the ones drawn by Claire in Figure 8.18. Another way is to express the child's links in words and compare them with the statements in the curriculum document for different levels of achievement.

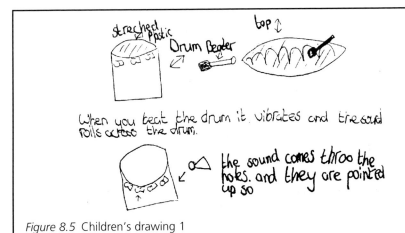

Figure 8.5 Children's drawing 1

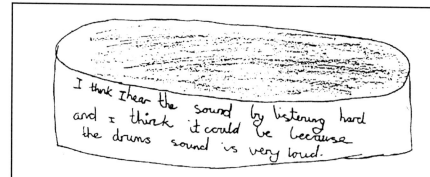

I think I hear the sound by listening hard and I think it could be because the drums sound is very loud.

Figure 8.6 Children's drawing 2

I noticed that when I plucked the rubber band it made a low noise. If I stretched the band tighter the pitch of the noise was higher. The more I stretched the higher the noise became.

(Age 9 years)

"I noticed that when I plucked the rubber band it made a low noise. If I stretched the band tighter the pitch of the noise was higher. The more I stretched the higher the noise became."

Figure 8.7 Children's drawing 3

'Things that give off light'

Figure 8.8 Children's drawing 4

Katrina – My feet are soft and pink underneath
The size of shadows change when you move the torch in and out
Talked freely about baby brothers

My foot wen I shind on my foot went diffrie and went
Smaller wen I mved in and out

This my foot

torch

Figure 8.9 Children's drawing 5

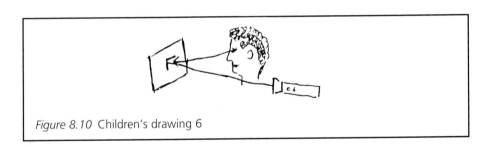

Figure 8.10 Children's drawing 6

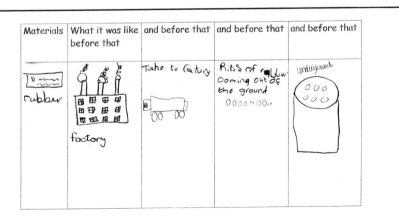

Materials	What it was like before that	and before that	and before that	and before that
rubber	factory	Turn of the Century	Bits of rubber Coming out of the ground 0000 00 00	Underground

Figure 8.11 Children's drawing 7

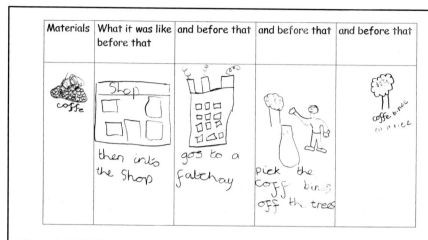

Materials	What it was like before that	and before that	and before that	and before that

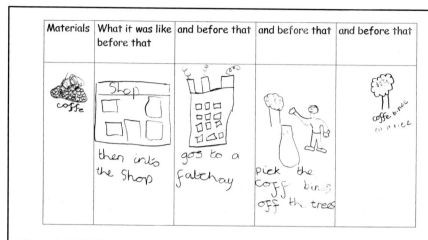

Figure 8.12 Children's drawing 8

Paper | used for writing on
it is a god material because
you would not have
any thing to write on.

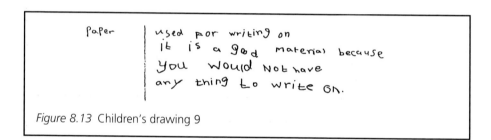

Figure 8.13 Children's drawing 9

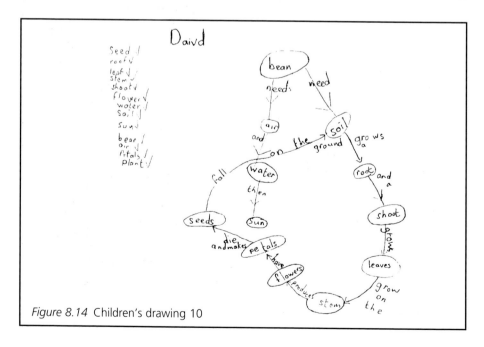

Figure 8.14 Children's drawing 10

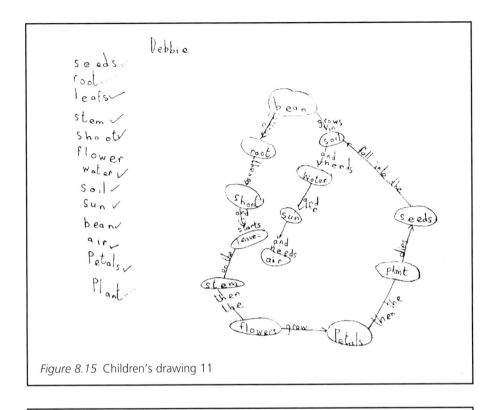

Figure 8.15 Children's drawing 11

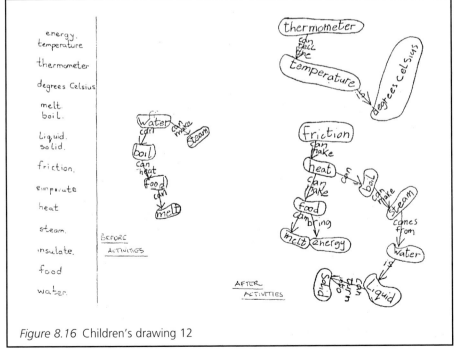

Figure 8.16 Children's drawing 12

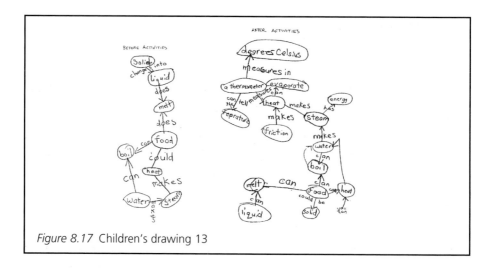

Figure 8.17 Children's drawing 13

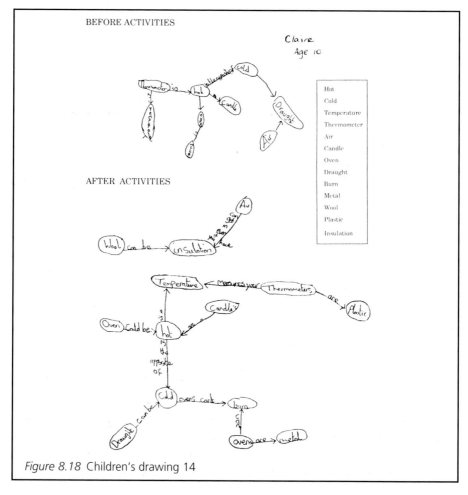

Figure 8.18 Children's drawing 14

DISCUSSION AND REFLECTION

Activity 1

You may like to compare your re-arranged list for 'processes of life' with the three groups that some teachers used in defining a progression, ideas for earlier, middle and later development as shown in Figure 8.19.

Reasons for placing ideas in these groups included that the later ideas required understanding of some earlier ideas (e.g. 'organs arranged in systems' requires understanding of the life processes). Other reasons became evident from contrasting earlier and later ideas for 'interaction of living things and their environment', as in Figure 8.20.

Consider these points:

- The early ideas are *descriptive* of experience, while the later ones embody explanations. That is, children can observe living things in their environment and as a result form these ideas. On the other hand, the 'later' ideas indicate an *explanation* of observations.

Earlier	Middle	Later
Living things produce their own kind There are different kinds of living things called plants and different kinds called animals, which include human beings	Animals and plants depend on each other in various ways Human beings need certain conditions to promote good health and body maintenance The basic life processes are common to plants and animals	There are organs within the bodies of mammals arranged in systems which carry out the major life processes All living things are made of cells

Figure 8.19 Development of children's ideas on living things

Early ideas	Later ideas
Changes occur in living things in response to daily and seasonal changes in the environment	Competition for life-supporting resources determines which living things survive where
Different plants and animals are able to live and find food in very different places	Plants are the ultimate source of food for all living things

Figure 8.20 Early and later ideas on interaction of living things and their environment

- The early ideas indicate that *simple patterns* have been identified by linking observations of two things together (e.g. difference in the living things and differences in time), while the later ideas require a more complex linking through several *chains of reasoning*.
- The early ideas are more observable and *'concrete'* while the later ones are more *abstract*.

How do these compare with the broad differences that you identified?

Note that the ideas listed here are not the small ideas that apply to particular living things. They are generalisations across living things. For young children these will necessarily be based on only a small number of observations, for example that worms are found in soil and are able to live there, while fish would not be able to live in soil but only in water. Thus, although the early ideas are not expressed as relating to particular living things, they are only a step away from the 'small' ideas that refer to specific objects or events. There is, therefore, a change from smaller to bigger ideas within the progression. Also, these generalisations about living things are, like all scientific generalisations, hypotheses that can never be proved 'right'. (See the quotation from Steven Hawking in Module 1 on p. 4). We have not yet found a living thing that does not 'produce its own kind' but there is always the possibility! Until that time we are happy to live with and use this idea because it is the best way we have for making sense of our present experience.

Activity 2

In looking at the examples of children's work and drawings you probably find that you often want to say that there is *some* evidence, but not enough to make a judgement about a child's understanding of the idea. Thus consideration of what the teacher needs to do to get more information is important. One way is to accumulate information over several occasions, when different specific objects are being investigated, for example, different musical instruments or different materials. Another way is to discuss the work with the child to probe the extent to which the ideas can be applied to other situations. All this is, of course, demanding of time. It raises the question about the trade-off between covering fewer concepts well or more concepts but more superficially. When there is a required curriculum to cover, this is not a matter that individual teachers are free to decide for themselves. However, within the curriculum it is possible to ensure that the balance of time spent on difference ideas favours the more important ones.

From the point of view of using written work and drawings to gather information about children's ideas, it is worth considering the way in which the task was given to the children. In several cases in these examples, the children were asked specifically to show or write about 'how you think you hear the drum' or 'how you think you see the light from a torch that is behind your head, using a mirror'. If the tasks had been given in terms of 'drawing a picture to show what you did', then the thinking might not have been revealed. So if we have a clear idea of the ideas we want to assess, the task should be set to ensure that children make their views explicit. Asking children to draw concept maps is one way of focusing very specifically on particular ideas.

Activity 3

You might like to compare your map with the one produced by some teachers, as shown in Figure 8.21. How easy do you find it to 'read' a map drawn by someone else?

You probably found that drawing a map made you think very hard about the relations between these concepts and the way in which they can all be interconnected. You may also have realised what you do not know about how some are related. If so, this demonstrates the value of drawing concept maps for assessing ideas. Of course, it is essential for the concepts mapped to be ones that you are familiar with and know something about. That is why it is usual, when using concept maps with children, to start by brainstorming the concept words that are to be included in the map. You may also have found the process easier, as do children, if the concept words are pasted onto card so that they can be moved around physically to bring linked ones close together.

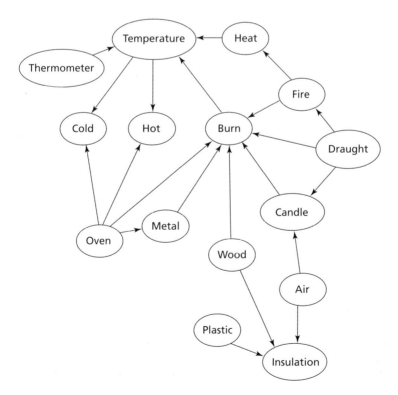

Figure 8.21 Completed concept map, without link labels

Activity 4

In this activity you will have considered various ways of using the information from children's concept maps. In the case of David and Debbie, it seems on first looking at their maps that they have already learned a good deal about the parts of plants and what seeds need to grow. They recognise that air is needed, something that is often overlooked by children. But they also include 'sun' as needed, and it is not clear, particularly in David's map, whether this refers to a bean plant or a bean seed. Also, Debbie seems to indicate that the plant dies in producing seeds. These may have implications for the next steps for these children, taking into account what they have already learned.

The 'before' and 'after' maps are useful for the teacher in giving information about what changes in ideas have taken place during the course of the intervening activities. The two separate parts of Kathy's and Claire's maps suggest that there is further 'linking' to be done, but perhaps this is as far as 6 year olds can be expected to go. Indeed, the maps show that these children have more advanced ideas than might otherwise have been expected or indeed revealed.

There is also considerable potential in 'before' and 'after' maps for indicating to the children themselves the progress they have made. An example of this self-assessment use is described in some detail by William Stow in an article in *Primary Science Review* (1997). He reported two main benefits from using concept mapping in this way. The first was motivational, for the children showed pleasure in seeing what changes had taken place and evidence of what they had learned. The second was the encouragement to 'think about their thinking' (meta-cognition). The mapping provided them with a way of analysing their ideas and identifying where their ideas had changed and what they were still unsure about. It also helped them to think about the words used in expressing and discussing their ideas.

Turning to the question of whether children have reached a particular level in conceptual understanding (as needed for summative assessment and reporting), how did your map, or the one given on page 121, compare with Claire's? In comparing any maps and particularly in comparing a map with a statement of attainment in the curriculum, it is often useful to turn parts of the map into a narrative. For example, Claire's map includes evidence that she has developed the idea that 'thermometers measure temperature which means how hot or cold things are'. This can then be compared with curriculum statements indicating various levels of working.

Finally, note that there are other ways of assessing children's understanding of ideas:

- Setting specific 'application' questions. It is important for these to seek application in a context different from that in which it was learned.
- Using concept cartoons (see Further Reading). These are enjoyable for children and teachers, but the ideas discussed are the ones presented and may not tap into the particular ideas that children have.
- Setting up a discussion among children and listening to the words they use and how they relate one idea to another (i.e. an oral concept map).

Concept cartoons can be used for this, especially if children are encouraged to add their own ideas to those given in the cartoon.

REFERENCE

Stow, W. (1997) 'Concept mapping – a tool for self-assessment?', *Primary Science Review* No. 49, pp. 12–15.

FURTHER READING

Atkinson, H. and Bannister, S. (1998) 'Concept maps and annotated drawings', *Primary Science Review* No. 51, pp. 3–5.
Cross, A. (1992) 'Pictorial concept maps: putting us in the picture', *Primary Science Review* No. 21, pp. 26–8.
Harlen, W. (2000) *The Teaching of Science in Primary Schools*, 3rd edn, London: David Fulton Publishers.
Kilshaw, M. (1990) 'Using concept maps', *Primary Science Review* No. 12, pp. 34–6.
Millar, L. and Murdoch, J. (2002) 'A penny for your thoughts', *Primary Science Review* No. 72, pp. 26–8.
Naylor, S. and Keogh, B. (2000) *Concept Cartoons in Science Education*, Crewe, Cheshire: Millgate House Publishers.
Willson, S. and Willson, M. (1994) 'Concept mapping as an assessment tool', *Primary Science Review* No. 34, pp. 14–16.

Module 9 Involving children in assessing their work

INTRODUCTION

The research review by Paul Black and Dylan Wiliam (1998) referred to in Module 6 found many studies that indicated the value, in the context of formative assessment, of helping children to assess their own work. At the same time they recognised some of the obstacles to the wider implementation of this practice:

> Many of the successful innovations have developed self- and peer-assessment by pupils as ways of enhancing formative assessment, and such work has achieved some success with pupils from age five upwards. This link with formative assessment is not an accident – it is indeed inevitable.
>
> To explain this, it would first be noted that the main problem that those developing self-assessment encounter is not the problem of reliability and trustworthiness; it is found that pupils are generally honest and reliable in assessing both themselves and one another . . . The main problem is different – it is that pupils can only assess themselves when they have a sufficiently clear picture of the targets that their learning is meant to attain. Surprisingly, and sadly, pupils do not have such a picture.
>
> (Black and Wiliam, 1998, p. 10)

The point to emphasise in this is that children do not have a clear picture of the intended *learning* from their work. For children *do* assess their own work, even though we and they may not be aware of doing this. The problem is that they do this without knowledge of what they should be learning. For example, when the PACE (Primary Assessment and Curriculum Experience) project asked children how they felt about their teacher looking at their work, some responses were:

If I've done something not quite right I feel nervous. We show each other our work. If theirs is better than mine I feel really worried.

I don't like giving my book in 'cause it's a mess – I hide it at the bottom of the pile.

Sometimes I don't want her to look at it because I haven't tried. I haven't put enough effort into it.

It depends what book she's looking at. I like it when she looks at my science and my English because I always get them finished – and maths. I don't like her looking at the rest.

These quotations indicate that children are making some judgement of their work, although they don't always know how the teacher will judge it. They are worried when they don't know the criteria the teacher will use. For example:

When I know I've done it right I feel good. When I don't know if I've done it right I feel worried.

Always worried at first. Sometimes you think you've done a really horrible piece of work and he says it's all right and you think 'phew!'

I'm actually kind of worried, nervous when I give work in at the end of the day . . . I don't know what's going to happen.

(quotes from Pollard and Triggs, 2000)

Across a large number of responses to this question the PACE researchers found that children generally judged their work in terms of its quantity, correctness, neatness, whether it was finished and how much effort was put in. These criteria were the ones they thought the teacher was applying, and they picked this up from what the teacher often commented upon. However, these were not necessarily the goals of the particular piece of work and it appeared that generally the children (years 5 and 6 in this case) were unaware of the *learning* that was intended.

This emerged also in a class which was observed as part of the Association for Science Education and King's College, London (AKSIS) project, when some boys spent three lessons finding out which of three kinds of paper was the strongest. Afterwards they were interviewed:

Interviewer: What do you think you have learned from doing your investigations?
Robert: . . . that graph paper is strongest, that green one.
Interviewer: Right, is that it?
Robert: Um . . .

Interviewer: You spent three lessons doing that, seems a long time to spend finding out that graph paper is stronger.

James: Yeah, and we also found which . . . paper is stronger. Not just the graph paper, all of them.

The boys appeared to be unaware of the process of investigation as a learning goal, in contrast with their teacher. It seems reasonable to assume that, had they been aware of this goal, they would have reflected more on the way they were investigating, found more satisfaction in the investigation and made more progress towards the goal that the teacher had in mind.

(Harlen, 2001, p. 132)

Children should know what the educational aims of their work are so that they can focus their effort and judge whether or not they are achieving them. Therefore in this module we start with the matter of sharing goals with children and then look at ways of involving children in self- and peer assessment.

Activity 1 is about finding the right words to use to communicate goals to children. Clearly this means using language appropriate for the age and maturity of the children. And, of course, stating the goal does not mean telling the children the specific idea or the conclusion that you hope they will reach. So, for instance, if the activity is to find out what keeps an ice cube from melting for the longest time, you don't say that the goal is 'to see that x is the best material for keeping the ice frozen'. Rather, you would indicate what they will learn *about*, or learn *how*. Activity 1 asks you to think about how to express goals in ways that children can understand and which tell them what they will learn, not what they will do. (You may have to tell children what they should do, but this should not be confused with sharing the learning that is the point of the activity.)

However, there are two aspects to communicating a learning goal: conveying the kind of learning and the quality of work that is expected. Activity 2 is concerned with the second of these. It provides an example of how a teacher helped her pupils to identify the aspects of a report of an investigation that make it a 'good' report. It is significant that this teacher involved the children in the process. They thought up the criteria for themselves and so that the criteria did not need to be explained, the pupils understood them from the start.

Knowing the goals and the quality criteria is essential to children being able to assess their own work. We are concerned here, of course, with formative assessment, that is, assessing to see what has been achieved and what are the next steps. Activity 3 presents five 'tried and tested' approaches to pupil self-assessment for consideration. In Activity 4 the discussion is extended to peer assessment, which has many benefits for pupils and enables them to assess their work without needing one-to-one interaction with the teacher, for which opportunities are clearly limited.

Activity 1

For the two activities given in Figure 9.1 and two more that you choose, write down what your goal would be for the children to learn and then how you would convey this to the children (please write the exact words you would use).

Activity and age group	Your learning goals	What to say to the children
Owl pellet dissection (age 8/9)		
Toy cars rolling down a ramp (age 6/7)		

Figure 9.1 Pro-forma: learning goals

Developing criteria for judging the quality of work

Here's how one teacher helped her class to identify what makes a good report of an investigation:

Mrs B gave each group of children two examples (presented anonymously) of accounts of an investigation written by children in the same class in earlier years. One was a clear account, well set out so that the reader could understand what had been done, although the writing was uneven and there were some words not spelled correctly. There were diagrams to help the account, with labels. The results were in a table, and the writer had said what he or she thought they meant. However, it was admitted that the results didn't completely answer the initial question and there was a comment about how things could have been improved. The other account was tidy, attractive to look at (the diagrams were coloured in but not labelled) but contained none of the features in the content shown in the other piece.

continued

She asked the children to compare the pieces of work and list the good and poor features of each one. Then they were asked to say what were the most important things that made a 'good' report. The class brainstormed their ideas and Mrs B collected them and later made copies for all the children to keep in their science folders. But she also went on to explore with the children how to carry out an investigation in order to be able to write a good report. These points too were brought together in the children's words and printed out for them.

Activity 2

Discuss in your group (or think about, if you are working alone):

(a)   How important is it for children to understand the criteria of quality of their work in science, as well as the learning goals?

(b)   What are the pros and cons of the method used by Mrs B? Would it be suitable for all age groups? Would it allow for a development in the expectations of quality as children get older?

(c)   What other ways have you used, or can suggest, for helping children to understand what is expected in terms of the quality of their work?

Encouraging children to assess their own work

Self-assessment is not something that can be introduced all at once to children who are not used to it. Shirley Clarke, in *Unlocking Formative Assessment* (2000), suggests starting with some questions displayed on the classroom walls to stimulate self-assessment at the end of lessons. These include: 'What do you need more help with about learning to . . . (whatever the learning goal was)?', 'What are you most pleased with about learning to . . . (learning goal)?' Clarke suggests, for one to three weeks, spending some time at the end of each lesson to model some answers children might give. After the modelling period, the teacher might choose one question, relate it to the learning goal of the lesson and give a period (15 to 30 seconds) for children to think about their answer. Then the teacher either collects responses in a whole class discussion or has the children working in pairs and exchanging their thoughts, or he or she discusses with a group at a time, while other groups do other things.

Clarke makes a useful point about encouraging self-evaluation by responding to children who say they were 'stuck' by welcoming this as an essential step in finding out how to help the learning. By the same token she suggests that a teacher might respond to children who find no problem by telling them that this is worrying because they may not be learning anything new. Activity 3 lists some other ways in which teachers have engaged children in self-assessment of their work.

Activity 3 Self-assessment

Some examples of approaches to self-assessment:

A   Selecting their 'best' work from their folder or note book and explaining to the teacher why these pieces have been chosen.

B   Taking any piece of work and answering the questions: 'What have I done well?', 'What could I have done better?', 'What do I need to do to improve?'

C   As B, but presenting this to their parents/guardians on parents' evening.

D   Asking children to set a task for their peers designed to show if they have understood a concept.

E   Using 'traffic lights', that is, children mark their own work in terms of their understanding, using a green spot if they are confident that they understand, yellow if they are not totally confident and red if they feel that they don't understand something about their work.

For each of these approaches to encouraging self-assessment and for others that you have used, decide the age groups and circumstances in which they may be most appropriate and suggest how they might be modified for other age groups, then complete Figure 9.2.

Approach	Age group and context suitability	Modification for other age groups and contexts
A		
B		
C		
D		
E		
Other		

Figure 9.2 Age group and context suitability

Activity 4

(a)   Which of the approaches in Activity 3 can be adapted to peer assessment? Can you add any other approaches to peer assessment from your experience?

(b)   In what circumstances (age group, context, purpose) is peer assessment appropriate? In what circumstances do you consider it would be inappropriate?

DISCUSSION AND REFLECTION

Activity 1

An obvious point that comes to the fore here is that the teacher has to be clear about the learning goals before thinking about how to share them with the children. Compare your answers about the owl pellets activity with these from various teachers, as shown in Figure 9.3.

Example	Teacher's learning goal	What to say to the children
Owl pellet dissection	The children will learn about the food of the owl.	What you will be learning is about what the owls eat.
	The children will experience an investigation where they can use evidence to draw conclusions.	In this activity you should try to work as a scientist, see what you find and then try to decide what it means.
	The children will add to their understanding of food chains and the interdependence of living things.	In this activity you will learn more about how one living thing depends on others.

Figure 9.3 Teacher's learning goal

There are pros and cons to all of these (we said it wasn't easy!). The first of the teacher's goals is the most straightforward, but it refers to the very specific learning from this activity rather than the 'big' idea, which is stated in the third of the teacher's goals. However, it is difficult to share the 'big idea' with children, as the example shows. Certainly the teacher might well have this idea in mind but for children of this age the immediate learning is about the owl's food. The second goal, which could be the main goal or an additional one, refers to the process rather than the product.

Activity 2

Most teachers answer the question about the value of children understanding criteria for judging quality in the affirmative, but with a caveat that it does depend on what the criteria are. There is a danger of reinforcing children's tendency to regard the surface and visual aspects of work as the most important, or to use criteria that are familiar in relation to their written work – good spelling, correct punctuation, and so on. So it is essential in using an approach such as Mrs B's that the children consider what the purpose of the work was and implicitly (but probably not explicitly) interpret quality as 'fitness for purpose'. So the relevance of the criteria to the science content should be foremost.

Among the 'pros' of Mrs B's method that have been suggested:

- it encourages children to look carefully at the work of others and learn to criticise constructively;
- the criteria they identify are ones that make sense to them and are already expressed in words they understand and the problem of explaining them to the children does not arise;
- the criteria are made public and help towards a spirit of 'learning together'.

Among the 'cons', in addition to the reservation mentioned above:

- the children might not 'believe' the pieces of work or not take them seriously;
- the criteria could be too rigorous or too lax;
- not all might agree with the criteria suggested;
- the meaning might be ambiguous.

The benefits and disadvantages clearly depend on how the teacher handles the discussion and in these points are indications of what to encourage and what to avoid. In particular it is important to encourage constructive, positive criticism.

The emphasis on being positive is the core of a variation on Mrs B's approach offered by another teacher. He arranged the 11 year olds in his class in pairs to look at one piece of work. They were asked to agree on three good points about the work and three things that could be improved. By careful whole class discussion he developed general criteria from the specific points they made. With these older children he was able to suggest additions which the children had not mentioned.

Activity 3

Approach A is suitable for all ages but is the most appropriate for young children or those just starting self-assessment. It is essentially about identifying criteria for assessment and these will be individual rather than shared in the class. But it is a starting point for an activity such as the ones described in B and C. If the discussion with the teacher takes place some time after the work was carried out, the child is more likely to be prepared to discuss improvements. The teacher can then ask 'You did this some time ago, do you think you could now make it even better?', 'What could you do to improve it?'

Approach B is valuable as long as it does not become part of boring routine. To avoid this it is important to ensure that there is time to discuss a piece of work thoroughly and to give the child the individual attention that the process needs. This means that it is only possible once in a few weeks rather than every week; but less frequent and more focused treatment is better than hurried and superficial attention. (This is where peer assessment can come in, to provide more opportunities for pupils to talk about their work to another.)

Approach C requires some preparation, particularly where children are new to this way of reflecting on their work. It may by helpful to 'model' the discussion of a piece of work in a way they could do with their parents. As part of preparing for a parents' evening, there could be some role play where children try out what they will say in pairs. This is a good use of time if it also helps the children to look more carefully at their work in relation to the criteria of quality.

Approach D is best used occasionally and with the assessment taking the form of a practical activity. For instance, in one class some pupils set up simple circuits that did not work and asked others to find out how to make them work. They were quite ingenious in concealing a piece of a non-conductor in the circuit – and by doing this they tested their own understanding of materials and circuits as well as that of their peers.

Approach E has been developed and used with lower secondary pupils, but has potential at the upper primary level. It requires some gradual introduction and possible modelling. The teacher might demonstrate what to do: 'Suppose I've finished the activity, and I read through what I've written and reflect on what I did. If there is something I'm not quite sure about then I put a yellow spot on the top corner. If I really don't understand, then it is a red one. But if I feel it all makes sense, then it is a green spot.' The teacher can explain that the spot is not a mark but a way of helping the teacher to know when to go on or to go over things. This approach is particularly applicable to the conceptual understanding in an activity and clearly requires a classroom climate where it is acceptable for pupils to discuss what they don't understand.

Activity 4

Peer assessment in the context of formative assessment means something quite different from children marking each other's books. In essence it means children helping each other with their learning, because formative assessment involves deciding and taking steps to take learning further.

One of the advantages of peer assessment, hinted at above, is that it requires less one-to-one attention from the teacher, which is required by several of the approaches to self-assessment discussed in Activity 3. Clearly, opportunities for this are limited. However, children can more frequently discuss their work with each other and help each other to improve. But teacher time is not the only reason for encouraging peer assessment. Having children talk to each other about their work requires them to think through the work again and find words to describe it without the pressure that comes from the unequal relationship between the child (novice) and the teacher (expert). It is also consistent with the understanding of learning as being the development of ideas through social interaction as well as through interaction with materials. It can help children to respect each other's strengths, especially if pairs are changed on different occasions.

The paired discussion needs to be structured, at least when it is new to the children. For example, the children can be asked to exchange work and then think about two or three questions about it reflecting the criteria of quality. For instance, if the work describes a conclusion from something that has been observed or found from an investigation, the questions might be 'Can you tell what was found?', 'Does the conclusion help to answer the question that was being investigated?', 'What would help to make it clearer (a diagram, or series of drawings)?' After such a discussion one child said about having her work assessed by another: 'She said it was hard to understand my investigation so I asked her what sort of thing I should have put to make her understand. Next time I will make sure that I describe things more clearly.'

This approach to peer assessment clearly requires a class atmosphere where cooperation and collaboration, rather than competition, are encouraged. When they have confidence in gaining help from a structured exchange with a peer, children begin spontaneously to ask each other for their opinion. The recognition of being able to help themselves and each other enables learning to continue when the teacher is occupied with those who need extra help.

REFERENCES

Black, P. and Wiliam, D. (1998) *Inside the Black Box*, London: School of Education, King's College, London.

Clarke, S. (2000) *Unlocking Formative Assessment*, London: Hodder and Stoughton.

Harlen, W. (2001) *Primary Science: Taking the Plunge*, 2nd edn, Portsmouth, NH: Heinemann.

FURTHER READING

Goldsworthy, A., Watson, R. and Wood-Robinson, V. (2000) *Investigations: Targeting Learning*, Hatfield: Association for Science Education. Publication of the AKSIS (Association for Science Education and King's College, London) project.

Pollard, A. and Triggs, P. with Broadfoot, P., McNess, E. and Osborn, M. (2000) *What Pupils Say: Findings from the PACE (Primary Assessment, Curriculum and Experience) Project*, London: Continuum.

Module 10 Providing effective feedback to children

INTRODUCTION

Feedback from the teacher on children's work has an important role to play in children's learning and in their view of themselves as capable and successful learners. There is much evidence that children base their view of themselves as learners and their likelihood of succeeding in the face of a new challenge, on the feedback they have from performance in similar tasks in the past. Feedback from previous success or failure accumulates to influence their future motivation for learning.

This is an important reason for ensuring that children are not continually faced with tasks which are too difficult. Learning steps should be large enough to challenge and maintain interest, but not so large that there is repeated failure. This is particularly relevant for low-achieving children, who, if they constantly fail to meet expectations, see themselves as unable to learn, and make no effort, thus making further failure almost inevitable. But it is also a reason for paying careful attention to the nature of the feedback children receive from their teachers. This teacher feedback has both a short-term and a longer-term effect. In the short term it contributes to the next steps in learning; in the longer term it contributes to the pupils' view of how successful they are in undertaking certain kinds of task. It follows that the nature of this feedback should support children's confidence in being able to learn, should not make them feel that they are failures but should show them how to make progress. It also lends weight to the importance of providing non-judgemental feedback in marking work.

This module is concerned with the nature of feedback to pupils and identifying the features of effective feedback. Feedback can only be effective if it is well informed. This may mean spending more time on looking carefully at what children have produced, or listening to what they say. Routine 'marking' can miss points that would give teachers help in identifying children's ideas and finding ways to assist their learning. When this happens, the process of marking may do little other than check that work has been done by children and may not always have a significant part to play in the children's learning. The module activities are designed so that you can consider how feedback can be more effective and thus make better use of the time spent on marking.

In order to consider the potential value of looking carefully at children's work, Activity 1 is a structured exercise in *describing* some work that children have done and suspending judgement until you are sure of the evidence on which judgements should be based. It should be emphasised that this is a professional development exercise and is not intended as suggesting that every piece of children's work can be considered in this way. However, the experience of doing this may well indicate that there is a great deal more in some work than might be noticed in 'a quick read' and that there is often useful information in children's work that goes unused. This raises issues of planning marking so that more attention can be given to some pieces of work than others. This is a matter we pick up later.

The exercise in Activity 1 is intended as a group experience. It is when we hear what others have noticed in a piece of work that we realise what we have missed. But if it is impossible for you to work with others, at least try to be disciplined about following the procedures, adapted for individual use. In other words, you will have to be your own 'chairperson' and your own time keeper. You need the following information about the context in which the work was carried out:

- Lee is 5 years old. The class was undertaking activities about feet after the teacher had read them a story called *Alfie's Feet* (by Shirley Hughes). In groups, the children were investigating different kinds of footwear to see if it was waterproof, drawing round their feet, measuring them, casting shadows of their feet and drawing the shadows. While Lee was investigating the shadow of his foot, his teacher noted that Lee 'noticed the concentric circle pattern made by the torch; noticed the size of the shadow changed when the torch was moved'.
- Tony is 10. His class had been studying various environments, including polar regions. They became very interested in how icebergs float. They floated some ice cubes in water and the teacher asked them to continue at home, using blocks of ice of different size and measuring the amount of ice above and below the water. Then they were asked to write up their investigation.

After reflecting on this experience you might use some of the same approach in Activity 2. These examples show teachers' feedback on the work and you are asked to consider your reactions to what the teachers wrote and then to decide what you would have done. More importantly, perhaps, is to consider why you responded to certain kinds of feedback in the way you did and why you prefer your alternative comments. What principles were underpinning your response? Try to list them, even if they are 'ideals' and you won't always be able to act upon them.

Activity 3 takes the discussion of feedback to the point of deciding the wording appropriate for particular work and particular children. Thomas's work in Figure 10.9 illustrates the drawings produced by the young children in the first set of work. In this case the feedback is oral, but try to identify the exact form of words you would use. For the second set of work, of 10 year olds, consider the written responses that you would make. Try to keep your principles in mind!

Activity 1

This is a structured exercise for professional development, not intended as a regular teacher activity.

(a) Work in groups of four. One of the group is nominated as the chairperson for the discussion. In this role he or she introduces the pieces of work, keeps time and makes sure that everyone makes a contribution. Each group follows these procedures:

1 The chairperson introduces the work and the procedures (2 minutes).
2 All read the work carefully in silence (3 minutes).
3 Each person has 2 minutes to describe what (s)he notices about the work.
4 The chairperson brings the points together as an agreed statement about the evidence.
5 Each person has 2 minutes to weigh what (s)he infers about the child's thinking – what is understood and what is not understood.
6 These ideas are brought together to consider what the next steps for the pupil might be.

Apply these procedures, first to the work of Lee (Figure 10.1) and then to that of Tony (Figure 10.2).

Figure 10.1 Lee's drawing of his foot

Activity 1 *continued*

Icebergs in water

Tony

Each time the iceberg floated with most of it under the water. It was only the surface above the water. I tried it with a flat circle, a round cylinder shape and a small ball of ice Each time mostly the same thing happened, it floated to the top with only the surface showing the rest was under the water.

I measured it with a tape measure.

The cylinder was 1 inch $\frac{1}{4}$ of that was above the water.

It was hard to measure it under the water.

Figure 10.2 Tony's discussion of icebergs

Source: *Primary Science*, No. 42, p. 2

(b) Finally, prepare to report on the experience of paying careful attention to the evidence before making inferences about the children's work.

Activity 2

Look at the examples of children's work in Figures 10.3, 10.4. and 10.5. The children were 8 or 9 year olds. They were exploring evaporation by leaving small quantities of various solutions exposed in the classroom and by putting wet paper towels in various places. The goal was to learn about water vapour in the air.

Last week the coffee was he dry it was wet but now it is dry up.

the coffee is dryed up and it looks liake toffe it has drayd up

Why has it dried up? I think because we left it for a week.

Where has the water gone? it has gone to the air

Figure 10.3 Child's view of evaporation 1

Activity 2 *continued*

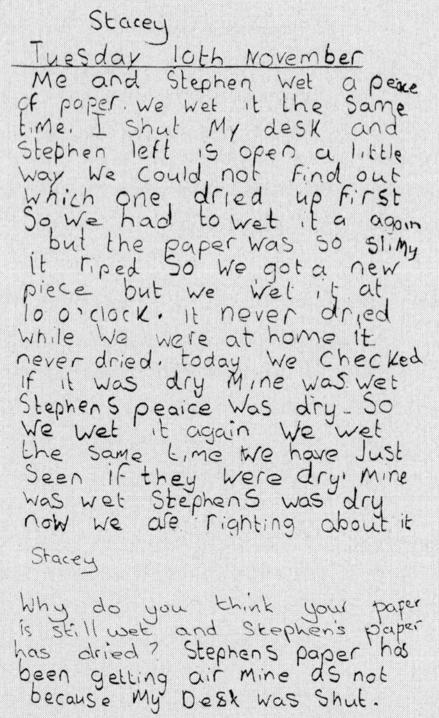

Stacey
Tuesday 10th November
Me and Stephen Wet a peace
of paper. We wet it the Same
time. I Shut My desk and
Stephen left is open a little
way We Could not find out
Which one dried up first
So We had to wet it a again
but the paper Was So Slimy
It riped So We got a new
piece but We Wet it at
10 o'clock. It never dried
While We were at home it
never dried. today We Checked
if it was dry Mine was wet
StephenS peaice Was dry. So
We Wet it again We Wet
the Same time We have Just
Seen if they Were dry Mine
was wet StephenS was dry
now we are righting about it

Stacey

Why do you think your paper
is still wet and Stephen's paper
has dried? StephenS paper has
been getting air mine as not
because My DeSk was Shut.

Figure 10.4 Child's view of evaporation 2

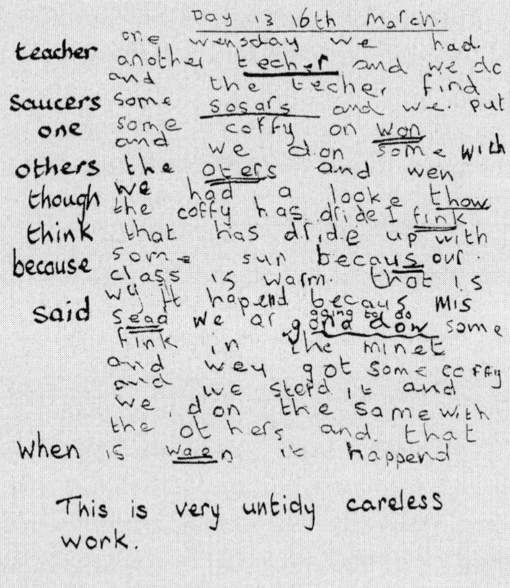

Day 13 16th March.
teacher one wensday we had
another teacher and we do
and the techer find
Saucers some sosars and we put
one some coffy on won
and we don some with
others the oters and wen
though we had a looke thow
the coffy has dride I fink
think that has dride up with
because some sun becaus our
class is warm. That is
said wy It hapend becaus Mis
sead we ar going to do some
fink in the minet
and wey got some coffy
and we sterd it and
we don the same with
the others and that
When is waen it happend

This is very untidy careless
work.

Figure 10.5 Child's view of evaporation 3

Activity 2 *continued*

(a)   Read carefully what the children wrote and the teacher's comments. Given the purpose of the activity, what is your view of the teacher's comments in each case?

(b)   How would you respond to this work? Complete Figure 10.6.

(c)   In your group, devise some guidelines for marking children's work so that the feedback helps their learning

	Comment on the teacher's response	The response you would give
Figure 10.3		
Figure 10.4		
Figure 10.5		

Figure 10.6 Response to children's work

Activity 3

For the two sets of work described below, use your 'guidelines for effective feedback' to decide how to respond, orally for the first set and in writing for the second set.

Set 1

Context: 6 and 7 year olds were investigating 'materials'. After a discussion about what their (wooden) chairs were made from and where that came from, tracing the wood back to trees, the teacher asked them to do the same thing for other objects: a handkerchief, a cup, a leather belt, etc. She suggested they could use books to find out what they didn't know.

The children drew a series of pictures (see Figure 10.7) and also wrote about each stage. Figure 10.8 shows what six children wrote by their drawings (the children's spelling has been corrected).

For each of these, write your own comments in Figure 10.9 and then what you would say to the children in response.

Activity 3 *continued*

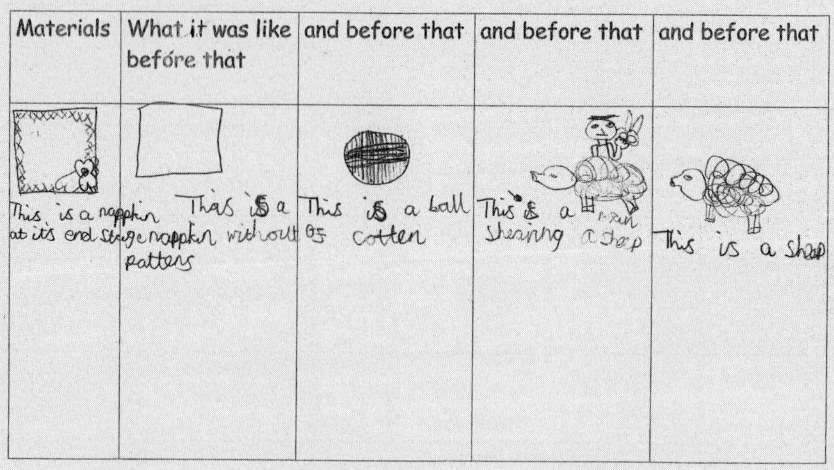

Materials	What it was like before that	and before that	and before that	and before that
This is a nappkin at its end singe patters	This is a nappkin without of	This is a ball of cotten	This is a man shearing a shep	This is a shep

Figure 10.7 Thomas's ideas about the origins of a handkerchief

	Object	What it was before that	. . . and before that	. . . and before that	. . . and before that
Thomas	Handkerchief	This is a handkerchief without its patterns	This is a cotton ball	This is a man shearing sheep	This is a sheep
Paul	Cup	Plain cup	Fire it in a kiln to make it hard	Clay	Dig clay from the ground
Lucy	Cotton cloth	Cotton thread	Cotton being cleaned	Cotton factory	A sheep
Katie	Leather belt	Strip of leather	Wash the skin	This is the skin of a cow	This is a cow
Elish	Cotton	A factory	Spinning wheel	Thread	A sheep

Figure 10.8 Children's views of changes in materials

Activity 3 *continued*

	Your comments/ interpretation	What you would say to the children
Thomas		
Paul		
Lucy		
Katie		
Elish		

Figure 10.9 Comments to children

Set 2

Context: the plans in Figure 10.10 were written by 11 year olds in answer to being asked what they would do to see which kind of container would keep soup hot for the longest time.

	'This is what I will do'	Your comments/ interpretation	What you would write in response
Mary	I would take some soup and pour it into the different cups and take the temperatures and see which was best.		
Daryl	I would take the three containers and fill each one with water at the same temperature and put lids on them all. I would put a hole in the lids and put thermometers through them. Then I would leave them and read the thermometers every minute. I would draw a graph of the centigrade at each minute.		
Yasmin	I would see how hot they were after a certain time. The best one would be the one that was hottest for the longest time.		

Figure 10.10 Children's views on keeping soup hot

DISCUSSION AND REFLECTION

Activity 1

Some observations

Lee has shown the relative positions of the torch, his foot and the shadow in a way which is almost three-dimensional (that is, the shadow is clearly on the other side of his foot from the torch). He labelled the parts of the drawing. Is the wavy line from the torch to the black spot on the foot an arrow or the line of the light? If the latter, why is it wavy? He noticed that the shadow was bigger than the foot, and, according to his teacher, that the size changed when the torch was moved.

Tony tried several differently shaped pieces of ice; he made measurements of how much of the cylinder of ice was above and below the water by measuring some distance. It is not clear what this was (vertical height?). He noticed that all the pieces of ice floated.

Some inferences

Assume that Lee was referring to the shadow when he wrote 'it made the foot go big' (or did he think the foot changed in size?). He has the torch, foot and shadow in the right sequence but not obviously in line. Next steps to see if he realises that the torch, object and shadow are in a straight line? Can he predict where the shadow will be if the torch is moved? etc.

Tony seems to have carried out the activity much as the teacher intended, but what is he learning from this? Does Tony equate the linear dimension of the ice with the volume of the object? What does he mean by surface, etc.? Possible next steps to think about why ice floats and compare the volume of a quantity of water before and after it is frozen.

More important than speculating about these particular cases – and we don't really know enough about the children to do more than speculate about next steps – is to reflect on the process:

- To what extent did the exercise change your insights into the children's work?
- What were your reflections on the process of considering pupils' work?
- What insights into these pupils' thinking might such study provide for their teacher?
- How likely is it that evidence of their thinking is available in children's work and remains unused?
- Are there any implications for routine marking, even though it is not possible to spend this amount of time on a regular basis looking at children's work?

Activity 2

The example in Figure 10.5 shows a very different approach from that used in Figures 10.3 and 10.4. The difference shows in the focus of the comments, which in the former are not focused on the science content of the work, but only on the appearance and spelling. This is a major distinction in approaches to marking.

Another important distinction, not represented in the examples, is between marking in terms of 'marks' or grades (8/10; B+ etc.) and marking in terms of comments. The effect of different feedback on pupils has been the subject of a number of research studies. In one of the best known of these studies, 10 and 11 year olds were randomly assigned to three groups given feedback in different forms. One group was given feedback given in the form of comments only, another was given feedback in the form of grades and the third was given both grades and comments. It was found that when children were working on tasks requiring divergent thinking, those who received comments only on their work scored more highly on subsequent tasks than those who received grades and those who received grades and comments. Also, the lower achieving children showed more interest in their work after receiving comments only. It appears that if there is a grade, which does not in itself help their learning, children do not take notice of the comments, which *can* help their learning. Thus if we wish feedback to help children, then we should give comments but not grade their work.

Other research shows that the kind of comment made also makes a difference. The important distinction is between non-judgemental and judgemental comments. Judgemental comments which tell the child how well he or she has done are seized upon in just the same way as are grades. These comments convey what the teacher thinks of the child's work and not what they now need to do. Even praise ('Good work', 'Well done, you tried hard') is not helpful to learning. Praise is a form of judgemental comment that has to be used discriminately if it is not to lose its effect. It makes children feel good, particularly if the praise is directed at the effort rather than the product. But praise alone will not advance children's learning. They also need to know how to direct this effort.

Consider these points in reflecting on what you think is good practice in marking. Then compare your list with these 'do's and don'ts' based on recommendations proposed by ex-HMI Neville Evans in an article in *Primary Science Review* (2001).

1 Plan the task for the children so that there are worthwhile learning outcomes.
2 Identify one or two aspects of the work that are of particular interest as the foci of the marking.
3 Comment only on the science-specific aspects of the work (unless the task was specifically set for careful presentation and accuracy in using language, for instance).
4 Avoid judgemental comments and, above all, scores, marks or grades, since these divert children's attention from what they have done.

5 Pinpoint weak aspects, such as misuse of terms or conclusions that are not based on evidence.
6 Don't pose rhetorical questions ('Do you think so?', 'I wonder why?').
7 By all means pose questions, so long as the child understands that a response will be expected and will be read.
8 Don't waste effort and time on marking tasks that are mainly about reinforcement.
9 Manage marking by clearly identifying what work is worth marking for its science. Any other work should be acknowledged by signature, not by the ubiquitous tick, which is often interpreted by pupils (and parents and others) as commendation.

When a teacher goes to the trouble of writing comments or posing questions that can take the children's thinking further, it makes sense to allow the children time to read and take note of the comments and answer any questions posed by the teacher. Goldsworthy *et al.* suggest one way of doing this:

> When you hand the work back allow pupils to work in small groups and ask them to look at one another's work and your comments. Ask them to work out what each of them needs to do to improve. You could try focusing on a group containing higher achievers, another average group and a group containing slower learners.
>
> (2000, p. 38)

This is an approach that is suggested with older juniors in mind, but the idea could well be adapted for younger children. Using marking in this way, as enabling a dialogue between teacher and pupils, increases the individual attention that each child receives. Expecting children to read their teachers' comments and giving them time to do this changes the role of 'marking' in teaching and learning. In fact it makes the label 'marking' seem very inappropriate. Hopefully we can see it as feedback into learning whatever the label.

Activity 3

In the examples, the children's spelling has been corrected, to avoid diverting attention from the science content.

You may be surprised at the prevalence of children's assumption that cotton comes from sheep. However, it seems more reasonable when we recall that (a) these children will be unlikely to have seen cotton growing and (b) we commonly use the term 'cotton wool', which seems designed to confuse cotton and wool! (As noted in Module 2, there is often a reason for children's ideas to be found in their everyday experience.) So the feedback should take this understanding of the children's own ideas into account. Since the feedback is oral, some teachers suggest that it could be accompanied by showing the children a book, such as 'The story of cotton', or by showing the children some sheep's wool and a picture of a cotton boll. 'Wool from sheep does look a bit like cotton, doesn't it? But they are different. Your woollen pullover comes from sheep's wool. Let's compare it with this cotton cloth . . .' Since there are several children with this misconception, the feedback can be to the group.

In the second set there are important differences between the children's work which will be reflected in the individual feedback. Note, for instance:

- that Daryl used water instead of soup;
- that Mary and Yasmin referred to soup, but would they really use it? Have they thought through their plans sufficiently?
- neither Mary nor Daryl has said how they would decide which was best;
- Yasmin has not considered how to set up a trial;
- none of them has mentioned that the quantities of soup or water need to be the same.

What other points did you notice? There may be so many points in some cases that the teacher would have to decide the most important in view of the goals of the work. To give too much feedback all at once can be as unhelpful as giving too little.

Finally, if this all seems to be too much, recall your guidelines for effective feedback and keep in mind that with marking, as with other aspects of education, 'less can mean more' – or mean better learning. A smaller quantity of work thoroughly considered is worth more than all work treated superficially. Often teachers feel obliged to put some mark on every piece of work because there is a strong expectation from parents and sometimes from the school management that all work has to be marked. However, schools are increasingly recognising the need to review marking practices, particularly in the light of the research that shows that many existing practices need to be changed. The purpose of the marking of children's work has to be carefully identified. Just as there are different aims of assessment, there are different aims of marking.

We have been considering here marking for helping learning, rather than for accountability. It is difficult to serve both purposes with the same approach to marking. That is why Neville Evans' suggestion (p. 144) of initialling some work (that was done for reinforcement) is worth considering. It would be important to explain this to the children and to their parents. The children would know that when there is detailed feedback they are expected to respond to it. Then the work put into marking is likely to lead to better learning.

REFERENCES

Evans, N. (2001) 'Thoughts on assessment and marking', *Primary Science Review*, No. 68, pp. 24–6.

Goldsworthy, A., Watson, R. and Wood-Robinson, V. (2000) *Investigations: Targeted Learning*, Hatfield: Association for Science Education. Publication of the AKSIS (Association for Science Education and King's College, London) project.

FURTHER READING

James, M. (1998) *Using Assessment for School Improvement*, Oxford: Heinemann.
Leakey, A. (2001) 'Fantastic feedback', *Primary Science Review*, No. 68, pp. 22–3.

Module 11   Science and other subjects

INTRODUCTION

This module is concerned with the links between science and other subjects. The focus is on the following:

- Planning in a more economical way for learning, using on occasions an integrated approach to achieving learning outcomes; linking subjects appropriately rather than in a way which loses the integrity of the subject.
- Identifying the opportunities for developing literacy and numeracy skills through science-based work.
- Helping children to see their learning in an holistic way.

In Activity 1 you will be able to consider how a story can be used as a starting point for cross-curricular planning. The learning experiences which can be planned using the story as a stimulus embrace many subjects and, as long as the teacher is quite clear about the learning objectives for each experience and keeps records of what has been done, then working in this way can be an enjoyable and worthwhile experience for the children.

Activity 2 is focused on citizenship which embraces topical issues, environmental issues and helps children to consider their place in society and their responsibilities to others. You will be asked to look at the science curriculum documents and to identify some areas which would provide a good context for citizenship. You will consider historical and topical issues and discuss environmental issues.

In Activity 3 there is an examination of how a study of the local area and in particular the roofs of buildings can help children to raise questions for scientific enquiry. The focus is quite clearly on the science but the stimulus of either a visit to observe buildings or research into the different types of homes around the world helps the teacher to plan for history, geography and science in an integrated way. Activity 4 is concerned with developing writing skills for a variety of purposes but the reasons for writing stem from science enquiries.

Activity 5 considers the use of non-fiction texts. Here the learning objectives are literacy-based but the content of the books is scientific and, while children are developing the writing skills, they will at the same time develop their scientific ideas. In Activity 6 you are asked to think about how measurement in science helps children to collect data which, when analysed, provides children with the opportunity to draw conclusions from their results.

Activity 1

A particularly effective way of approaching science for younger children is through the medium of stories. These can be used as a stimulus in part for older children, but care needs to be taken to ensure that the science is not lost or links contrived.

Read the story 'Polly and Humpty' used by some teachers of 5 and 6 year olds.

Polly and Humpty

One day Polly and her friend Humpty decided to go for a picnic. They were staying at the seaside for their holidays and Polly thought that the sea looked exciting.

She had seen the boats bobbing up and down in the water and had watched the children laughing as they put their hands into the water and splashed their fingers.

'Let's go for a sail and take a picnic,' Polly said to Humpty.

'Oh, yes, but please can we row the boat?' asked Humpty.

'Row the boat?', said Polly 'What do you mean . . . row the boat?'

'I want to pull the oars like the big girls and boys do,' said Humpty. 'That makes the boat go along in the water.'

'Oh that!' replied Polly. 'Of course you can. I want to put my fingers in the water and splash and splash,' she said jumping up and down.

'Come on, then, let's make some sandwiches and then we can go and get a boat.'

Polly and Humpty made some jam sandwiches and got two cans of Coke and four chocolate biscuits from the cupboard in the kitchen.

They put the food and drinks in a plastic coolbox with some blocks of ice and set off for the beach to see the man who looked after the boats.

They had to pay £1 for the boat and Mr Salty, the man who looked after the boats, told them to bring the boat back after one hour.

'Oh yes, we will,' said Polly, 'We only want to sail a little way and eat our sandwiches.'

Mr Salty gave them some little red jackets to put on. The jackets had air inside them just like balloons, and were to keep them from sinking if they fell into the water.

Polly and Humpty got into their boat. Humpty felt very important because he was using the oars, and he told Polly to sit very still in case she fell out.

Polly trickled her fingers in the water and sang a song. Humpty was very tired so he closed his eyes and went to sleep. Polly had a rest too, because the sun had made her sleepy. The little boat floated away on the sea, and Humpty and Polly slept on and on.

'Ummmm!' said Polly.

Activity 1 *continued*

'Ooh!' said Humpty.
'Snnnzz', snored Humpty.
'Snnnzz', snored Polly.
Suddenly there was a crash and a bump. They both woke up. Humpty looked around. Polly looked around.
'Where are we?' said Polly.
'Where are we?' said Humpty.
The little boat was not in the sea any more. It was stuck in the sand and had a hole in the bottom.
Humpty and Polly could not see any people. They could see some sand. They could see the sea. They could see a big hill made of sand, but they couldn't see any people. They were on an island.
Humpty began to cry. 'Oh, I want to go home,' he cried. He didn't feel important any more and wished that he hadn't decided to go for a sail. Polly didn't want her friend Humpty to feel sad so she tried to be brave. She went to look at the boat. There was a big hole in the bottom, but the sandwiches were still in the coolbox and so was Mr Salty's big toolbox and rope.
'Let's climb the hill and see what is on the other side,' said Polly. 'There may be some people there.' So Humpty and Polly climbed the hill. On the other side there were some trees, and hanging on the trees were some juicy oranges. There were no people to be seen.
'Well,' said Humpty, 'we could build a little house on this side of the hill and we have oranges to eat. I like oranges.'
'Oh yes!' said Polly, 'We'll be quite safe here and someone will be sure to find us. It will be an adventure, won't it?'

Consider how this may be used in a cross-curricular approach. Which curriculum areas could be covered? List some possible learning outcomes for each area.

Activity 2

PSHE has always had an essential role in primary education; however, the aspect of Citizenship has received increased emphasis, particularly with its statutory introduction at Key Stages 3 and 4.
The following is an extract from the National Curriculum *Handbook for Primary Teachers: Key Stages 1 and 2*:

Key Stage 1

Pupils should be taught:

- to take part in discussions with one other person and the whole class
- to take part in a debate about topical issues
- to realise that people and other living things have needs, and that they have responsibilities to meet them

Activity 2 *continued*

- what improves and harms their local, natural and built environments and about some ways people look after them
- to realise that money comes from different sources and can be used for different purposes.

Key Stage 2

Pupils should be taught:

- to research, discuss and debate topical issues, problems and events
- that there are different kinds of responsibilities, rights and duties at home, at school and in the community, and that these can sometimes conflict with each other
- to reflect on spiritual, moral, social and cultural issues, using imagination to understand other people's experiences
- to resolve differences by looking at alternatives, making decisions and explaining choices
- that resources can be allocated in different ways and that these economic choices affect individuals, communities and the sustainability of the environment
- to explore how the media present information.

Look at your curriculum for science and identify some areas that would provide a good context for the development of skills in citizenship. Try to draw on historical as well as topical issues, since history does on occasion repeat itself, particularly with respect to environmental issues, and this may be an area for looking at how scientific ideas are based upon evidence.

Activity 3

(a)   Look at Figure 11.1 and write down as many questions suggested by the picture which could be answered by scientific enquiry. Concentrate particularly on the roofs.
(b)   Consider how children might answer these questions by practical activity.
(c)   Be prepared to discuss these ideas and to identify the opportunities for learning science.

Activity 3 *continued*

Figure 11.1 Micklands houses' roof line

Source: Sue Malvern

Activity 4

Imagine that you are the teacher of 7 and 8 year olds who are learning about the properties of materials. Fill in the pro-forma in Figure 11.2 to provide examples of how science observations and investigations can be used to develop writing skills.

Type of writing	Science context
Sequencing events	
Writing instructions	

Activity 4 *continued*

Type of writing	Science context
Writing verses	
Preparing glossaries	
Letter writing	
Note making	
Writing stories	
Writing in charts and tables	
Describing events or observations	

Figure 11.2 Pro-forma: types of writing in science contexts

Activity 5

You have a non-fiction science book. Look at the title of the book but don't open it! In the first column of the pro-forma in Figure 11.3 write down all you know about the area of science which is included in the title of the book. For example, it could be snails or forces or the moon. When you have completed this, then identify in the second column what you would like to find out. When this column is completed, then you can use the book to find the answer to your questions.

Think about the strategies which you are using as you search for the information which you need.

What I know about	What I would like to know about	What I have learned about ......

Figure 11.3 Pro-forma: What I know, want to know and have learned

Activity 6

Mr Jones and his class of 9 year olds are learning about sound. They will be finding out whether children or adults have the best hearing and making and testing ear trumpets and trying to find out if ear trumpets help us to hear.

Identify the opportunities for the use of measurement as the children carry out the investigations.

DISCUSSION AND REFLECTION

Activity 1

Possible areas that may arise from reading the story are as follows:

Science

- Properties of materials, wet and dry sand, materials for the shelter and boat, waterproofing, similarities and differences.
- Healthy eating – what makes a healthy diet? Is the picnic they put together healthy?
- How quickly do different blocks of ice melt? Wrapping ice cubes in different materials to compare how quickly they melt.
- Comparing different boat shapes or sail shapes to see which moves fastest.

PSHE

- Empathy, understanding feelings, caring for others.
- Consider the dilemmas of the characters. What are their needs? How do they feel?
- Have the children ever felt like this? What did they do?

English

Any story has the potential to be used in many ways, so any list here would be extensive. One possibility to link with the PSHE would be to look at adjectives that describe feelings.

Design Technology

- Building a shelter, repairing the boat, making a smaller raft from the original boat.
- Can children design and make an island in the sand tray? What would the island need?
- Methods for attracting attention of other boats.
- Following on from healthy eating in science, designing and making sandwich fillings.

Mathematics

Measuring.

Geography

- Draw a map of the island from the description.
- Mark on the map the features described in the story.

The possible learning outcomes from the story are as follows:

Science

- Pupils are able to recognise common materials and understand why they are chosen for particular purposes.
- Pupils are able to describe some similarities and differences between materials, e.g. wet and dry sand.
- Pupils are able to use scientific terminology to describe materials, e.g. rigid, flexible, strong, waterproof.
- Pupils understand that eating the right kind of food helps to keep us healthy and which food should be eaten less often and why.
- Pupils can explain that ice melts when left at room temperature, and that some materials are more effective than others at keeping things cold.
- Pupils know that different shapes of boat travel at different speeds.
- Pupils know that sail size and shape can affect how fast a boat can travel.

The investigation using boats could result in the acquisition of many enquiry skills, as could that on the insulating properties of materials.

PSHE

- Pupils recognise the need to care for each other.
- Pupils learn to work co-operatively.
- Pupils are able to recognise feelings and learn how to cope with them.
- Pupils recognise that we all have different talents and how each person can contribute.

English

Pupils have an increased range of vocabulary to describe feelings.

Design Technology

The activities again give rise to a range of learning outcomes including:

- the ability to generate ideas;
- communicating their ideas by drawing and making models;
- selecting tools and materials;
- measuring, cutting and shaping materials;

- joining and combining materials in different ways;
- using finishing techniques;
- the hygiene procedures associated with preparing food;
- talking about their ideas and saying what works well and what they would change.

The activities give the opportunity to work with a range of materials including food and textiles.

Mathematics

- Pupils measure using non-standard or standard units.
- Pupils choose suitable measuring instruments.
- Pupils read the scales to the nearest labelled division with appropriate accuracy.

Geography

- Pupils are able to ask geographical questions.
- Pupils are able to express their views about the island environment.
- Pupils can make maps.
- Pupils can use geographical vocabulary.

Activity 2

Since 'science' often has a 'bad press', it provides a fruitful area for controversy – genetic engineering, cloning, depleting the Earth's resources, polluting the atmosphere – the list continues. How much of this is science rather than applied science or technology, or economics is debatable, however, since a degree of comfort has become the norm for significant proportions of the globe, many do not understand the cost of these, the implications for their continued avail-ability, and would not wish their comforts to be removed. The other side of the 'bad press coin' is exactly that, the benefits which accrue from scientific endeavour in prolonging life, relieving suffering, improving standards of living and leisure.

At an early age children can understand the needs of living things, including themselves. They are particularly quick to identify with environmental issues – the threat of pollution, litter and threats to species.

Even young children can study through other subjects, e.g. geography and history, the lifestyle of children in other countries and in other times. They can understand the need for an adequate and varied diet and as they get older, the importance of particular types of food. They can compare life in previous times with life now, including the quality of life for children, what they were expected to do in terms of child labour and the conditions in which they lived. They can discuss the introduction of medicines. Poor sanitation and the lack of clean water, and low levels of rainfall can all be related to the need to care for people on a global scale. Filtration, water treatment, evaporation and condensation will all arise. Flooding, both in England and elsewhere can be discussed, along with what can be done to alleviate suffering.

In discussing changes in materials, burning, and in particular the burning of forests, can be discussed and the impact upon the climate and local economy. Local issues, such as the siting of a landfill site or factory, can provide useful material for debate on the environment. How the media report on scientific and environmental issues can be examined.

Activity 3

Although in many schools the older children have separate lessons for history, geography, science and other areas of the curriculum, teachers often make links between subjects so that children can see their learning as an holistic experience. In a study of the local area this is particularly appropriate. In the case of Mickland School, Caversham, the Micklands estate is an easily recognisable enclave (see Figure 11.1). The houses of Micklands are easily identifiable because of the distinctive feature of the sharply angled roof line.

As you would expect, an area where the houses are noticeably unique has an interesting history. The estate was founded in the 1930s by a movement of labour from Wales under the Land Development Association and many local people remember calling it the 'Welsh Colony'. The design of houses in a particular area is often influenced by the people who first settled there. When we study the history and geography of any local area, the buildings provide a stimulating starting point.

The roof lines of buildings in various locations can provide not only a link to the history of the area but also to the geography. The climate of the country and the type of terrain have an influence on the design of the buildings. In Malta people are encouraged to build houses with flat roofs so that they can place water-collecting tanks there and, in places which have a great deal of snow, houses have particularly steep pitched roofs so that the snow will slide off.

Teachers should encourage children to be curious and to ask questions which they can investigate. This is true whether the questions are of a geographical, historical or scientific nature.

In this activity, you were asked to look at a photograph of some houses and to think of questions which might be answered by scientific enquiry. Children who raise these questions would be encouraged to find out answers for themselves and these answers might help them to understand why certain materials are used for a variety of purposes and why buildings are designed in particular ways.

Observation of the photograph will reveal:

- steeply pitched roofs and a flat roof over the garage extension;
- a 'lean-to' roof at the side of one of the houses.

Questions which may be raised might be:

- What happens to rain and snow when they fall onto the roofs?
- Why do houses have gutters?
- Why are flat roofs covered with roofing felt?
- Are 'flat' roofs really flat or do they have a slight slope?

Investigations which might be carried out by practical activity:

- Make model houses from shoe-boxes. Make some with flat roofs, some with slightly sloping roofs and some with steeply sloping roofs. Cover the roofs with plastic film and test to see what happens when simulated snow made from tiny polystyrene balls, which can be collected from packaging material, is dropped onto the roofs.
- Do the same with 'rain' produced by pouring water from a watering can.
- Observe roofing felt and try to make a similar product with a variety of materials. Test to see which of the home-made roof coverings are the most waterproof.

Perhaps you might have considered taking children out into the local area and giving them the opportunity to observe roofs. They will then be able to observe the different types of roofing tiles. Old houses may have slate roofs but most modern houses have tiles which are made of concrete. Building suppliers may be able to provide small samples of these materials for children to observe and to test for strength and porosity.

If it is possible to view a house under construction, then children can prepare sketches such as the one in Figure 11.4 which will help them to think about how the roofs are joined to the buildings, how the tiles are attached to the rafters and how the fascia board and the soffit board support the gutters. A collection of materials which are used in the construction of roofs can very often lead to further questions for investigation.

Children can be encouraged to carry out research into the types of materials used for gutters. In the lifetime of their great-grandparents and grandparents there will have been wooden gutters, metal gutters and plastic gutters and the reasons for the changes are nothing to do with fashion but to do with the availability of new materials and their properties. Perhaps children could find out for themselves that plastic will not rust or rot.

Possible learning outcomes of these experiences might be (see Module 1):

- to predict what might happen;
- to plan and carry out a fair test;
- to make relevant observations;
- to interpret evidence and to draw conclusions;
- to compare materials on the basis of their properties;
- to understand how the design of a house is influenced by the weather.

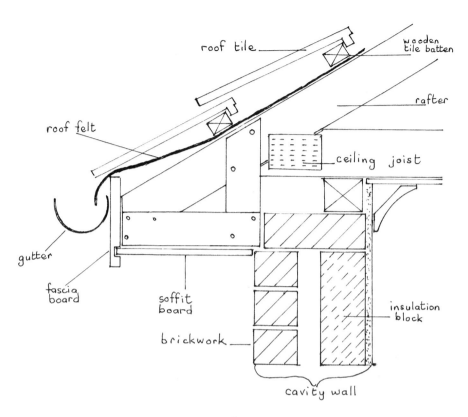

Figure 11.4 Sketch of cross-section of a roof

You might want to extend the study to include a consideration of the design of other homes. Older children could be encouraged to use the Internet to search for images of different types of houses and there could well be some discussion with your pupils about how the design is influenced by the climate in different places. If you consider the need to collect rainwater in Malta, there could well be some investigation into the best materials for making a water storage tank and the best shape for the tank.

Perhaps children could be asked why they think that the walls of houses in very hot countries are often painted in very light colours and whether or not cave dwellers would be hot or cold in their caves. Questions of this type can be answered by carrying out practical investigations and yet help children to understand the influence which the weather has on our lives. Further research about the natural resources of a geographical region might also lead to some ideas about why homes are built using certain materials.

Activity 4

Numeracy and literacy links

No-one would dispute that if children are to take their place in society, then the skills of literacy and numeracy are very important. However, there are many ways in which literacy and numeracy skills can be developed while at the same time providing children with opportunities to develop scientific ideas.

There are three activities in this section. The first part focuses on the different forms of writing with which children need to be familiar and the second part on the way in which information books about science can be used. The final part considers measurement in science.

Type of writing	Science context
Sequencing events	Make a flow chart to show the sequence of events when you carried out an investigation into which fabric was the most waterproof.
Writing instructions	Make chocolate crispy cakes and observe the changes as the chocolate melts and hardens. Write a series of instructions so that someone else can make the cakes.
Writing verses	Imagine that you are a sugar lump which has been put into a cup of hot water. Write a verse to describe how you feel and what happens to you.
Preparing glossaries	Prepare a glossary including words such as melt, dissolve, separate, etc. and explain the meanings.
Letter writing	After an investigation to find the most absorbent paper towel, write to the headteachers of the school requesting that the 'best' brand be used in the school cloakrooms.
Note making	Read non-fiction books about rubber, cotton or silk and make notes from a variety of sources.
Writing stories	Imagine that you are a candle on the dining room table. You are smart and red. Write a story about what happens to you as you burn away. Think about the colours in your flame and what happens to you when a boy in the house blows out the flame.
Writing in charts and tables	Make water filters from sand, paper, gravel and pebbles. Test out the filters as you try to clean dirty water. Write down the results of your observations in a chart.
Describing events or observations	Write a descriptive account – what you observe when you put ice cubes into a shiny can.

Figure 11.5 Examples of writing in science contexts

You will have suggested in Activity 4 a variety of ways in which children's writing skills can be developed as they think about and record their science investigations and observations. It is important that we are very clear about the learning objectives of the lessons. Some might be science-focused and the writing will be a way of reinforcing understanding of the science ideas or a means of recording results. At other times the main focus will be on developing the skills of writing using a science-based context.

Perhaps the ideas which you have suggested are similar to those in Figure 11.5.

Activity 5

In Activity 5 you will have been thinking about the strategies you used when you were looking for information in non-fiction science texts. How did you find the information? Did you use the contents page, the index or the glossary? If you were carrying out this type of activity with children, the learning objectives would be literacy-based but, nevertheless, just as you found out the answer to some scientific questions, so the children would be finding out answers to their own questions.

Activity 6

Activity 6 was concerned with measurement in science. Spence (1998) suggests that being numerate involves 'gathering numerical information by measuring and being able to present this information in graphs, charts and tables'.

Doing science investigations usually involves the collection of data. Sometimes this is collected by observing such as when we describe the results of decay after certain periods of time but very often some form of measurement is involved. By helping children to understand that accurate measurements will help them to answer questions which they want answered, we are making mathematics real and worthwhile. Children also need to be able to estimate and to think about whether their results are realistic. This, too, is an important part of helping children to solve problems accurately. Many young children are taught to repeat their measurements two or three times in order to make sure that they are accurate and teachers will help children to see the links between the maths which they meet in numeracy lessons and the mathematics which is used in science.

You were asked to consider the ways in which measurement is used when children are carrying out some investigations as part of their study of sound. They were investigating to find out if adults or children have the best hearing and about the effectiveness of ear trumpets.

Perhaps you have thought about how you would carry out this investigation with children as you need to do this before you can identify the measuring skills which will be used. Teachers have to make sure that children are not asked to use mathematical skills in science with which they are unfamiliar. The emphasis here is on using the skills which children have learnt in their mathematics lessons in a meaningful way. Here are some possible ways of carrying out the investigations.

Finding out whether children or adults have the best hearing

The teacher will discuss with the children how they might find out the answer to this question. Probable suggestions might include dropping a small object such as a paper clip onto a hard floor. People should be blind-folded and should stand with their backs to the person doing the dropping and raise their hand if they hear a sound. The children will need to decide whether the people being tested should move away from the 'dropper' or whether the dropper moves away from the people being tested. They will also have to make decisions about how far away from the sound source people should be each time they are tested. Would this be every metre, every 50 cms or less? The person with the 'best' hearing would be the person who could hear when they are a long way from the source and when all the other people being tested had failed to hear the object drop.

Children and their teacher would also need to discuss how results would be recorded and design a chart to show results.

Making and testing ear trumpets. Do ear trumpets help us to hear better?

Teachers will probably want to help children towards an understanding of how quantitative data can help us to interpret results and draw conclusions. The teacher in this example might give the children the opportunity to talk about how they might answer the question and there will probably be some discussion about why ear trumpets might have been used in the past and why they might be thought to be effective. Perhaps the teacher could show a picture of an ear trumpet, as it would be most unlikely that children would be familiar with them.

The suggestions for answering the question might involve making ear trumpets of different length or of different diameters and testing these in a controlled way. The children would have to measure the diameters and the length of the trumpets and also decide what to measure in order to judge which was most effective. This could involve measuring distances from a sound source in a similar way to the previous investigation, although the course participants might have other ideas.

The main points here are that children should be encouraged to use measurement in science and to understand how numerical data can help us to draw conclusions.

REFERENCES

National Curriculum Handbook for Primary Teachers: Key Stages 1 and 2, (1999)
London: DfEE/QCA.

Spence, M. (1998) 'Measurement in primary science and maths', *Primary Science Review*, No. 53, p. 6.

FURTHER READING

Feasey, R. and Gallear, R. (1999) *Primary Science and Literacy*, Hatfield:
Association for Science Education.

Feasey, R. and Gallear, R. (2000) *Primary Science and Numeracy*, Hatfield:
Association for Science Education.

QCA (2002) *Citizenship: A Scheme of Work for Key Stages 1 and 2*, London: QCA.

Module 12 Planning for continuity and progression in science activities

INTRODUCTION

This module provides opportunities to consider the importance of making provision for curriculum continuity, for progression in learning and for individual differences in your planning for work in science. Although the preoccupation of teachers is often: 'What will the children *do*?', this module is designed to encourage thinking about the process of planning, starting with questions about what the children might *need*, and *why*.

The words 'continuity' and 'progression' are sometimes used as if they are synonymous. It is worth exploring their interpretation, for teaching and learning. Although the meaning and the implication of each word are different, the words are strongly linked in the context of planning. Both continuity and progression apply to planning for conceptual understanding and for skill development. Continuity applies to provision and is important between schools and between classes in a school. In this module, we concentrate on within-school continuity. It is assumed that teachers' normal practices derive from a whole-school plan of work. Issues about liaison, for curriculum continuity purposes, between schools are not specifically addressed here.

Continuity is important in curriculum provision; in other words, the learning opportunities that children experience. Continuity is important to avoid repetition. Nothing is wrong with 'something completely different', but it is important to make references to and link it to work that has gone before. Progression applies to learning. It can be appropriate to plan for reinforcement of ideas or skills but steps in learning can be planned to broaden understanding and thus extend the skills repertoire. However, it is important to ensure that the 'steps' are of an appropriate size, according to needs of individuals. Differentiation, then, is important in ensuring that the planned progression is appropriate for individual children.

The importance of continuity in curriculum provision is not, of course, unique to science. However, as science is, by its nature, a practical subject, it is important for teachers to structure learning opportunities, through their plans for topics or themes, such that children are not bored, either by apparent repetition or through a perceived irrelevance of the work. It is possible for work in the same conceptual area to be planned for different purposes either to suit children with different levels of understanding or to challenge an idea held by a particular child, or to practise a particular skill. The implication here is, clearly, that teachers need to know what has gone before, for the children, and also need to acquaint themselves with children's individual achievements.

Finally, since teaching does not always lead to learning, there is a constant need for assessment and review.

Activity 1 presents a vignette which describes, in detail, aspects of one teacher's work. Analyse this in order to identify what considerations were important, as the teacher began to plan for activities and anticipate learning outcomes. These considerations are summarised as a series of steps in a planning framework. In Activity 2, you apply this framework to planning for work on 'keeping fit'. Activity 3 invites you to reflect on your plans. This opportunity for self-evaluation is facilitated by a number of focused questions. You might want to involve a colleague (a 'critical friend') here.

Activity 1

The vignette describes a teacher's approach to planning a series of science activities.

Chris was introducing science activities within an overall topic about growing food, to a class of 9 and 10 year olds. The previous year, the group had studied germination and plant growth, as part of their work in science. Chris planned that the children should discuss and investigate the differences between types of soil. The idea was that the children should undertake some investigations of sandy, loamy and clay soil, so samples of each of these were provided, to which some of the children contributed samples that they brought from gardens at home. Chris wanted the investigations to advance the children's ideas and therefore to start from their ideas and questions. It would have been easy to ask the children to find out, for example: 'Which soil holds most water?', 'Does water drain through some soils more quickly than others?', etc. and to start the children's investigations from these questions. These are perfectly good questions for children to investigate and likely to be among those the children ended up investigating, but Chris wanted to hold back such questions, in order to try to find out what the children would ask and what ideas they had.

The first part of the work was an exploratory phase of looking at the different soils. In groups, the children were given samples of the three main types, some hand-lenses, sieves, disposable gloves and some very open instructions:

- Separate the different parts that each of the soils contains.
- Find out what is contained in all the soils.
- Find out what is different in each soil.

Activity 1 *continued*

- Think about how these differences might affect how well plants grow in the soils.

This task required children to use their ideas about soil in making their observations. It encouraged them to look closely at the soil and to think about the differences they found. During this activity the teacher visited each group to listen in to what the children were saying about the types of soil. Many of their statements at this stage contained hypotheses and predictions. The children were quick to say which they thought would be best for plants to grow in (for example: 'The darkest coloured one') and to identify the ability to hold water as a property that was needed.

There was then a whole class discussion, pooling findings and ideas from different groups. Chris said that they would test their ideas about which was best for growing plants when they had found out more about the soils and the differences that might make one better than another. What do plants need to grow? Water was the most popular answer. Some mentioned 'fertiliser' and there was a discussion of what this meant in terms of the soils they had looked at and it was eventually identified with the bits of leaves and decayed plant material they had found, particularly in the loam. Chris introduced the word 'humus' to describe this part of the soil. No-one mentioned the presence of air in the soil until the teacher asked them to think about the difference between soil that was compressed and the same soil in a loose heap. They were challenged to think about whether there was the same amount of air between the particles in each soil and whether this was likely to make a difference to how well plants would grow in it.

The discussion identified four main differences to be investigated: the differences in the amount of water held in the soil; how quickly water drained off through each one; the amount of humus in each; and the amount of air. Each of the six groups in which the children were working chose one of these and set about planning how they would go about their investigation. Although having different foci, the investigations of all the groups were relevant to developing understanding of the nature and properties of soil so that, when they did the trial of which soil enabled plants to grow best, they would be able to explain and not just observe the result. Chris monitored how the children were working together in their groups: there were some who were inclined to 'take a back seat' and one or two who would rather be a scribe than participate in any practical work.

The investigations provided opportunities to help the children develop their enquiry skills, in order to carry out systematic and fair tests through which they would arrive at findings useful in developing their ideas. The teacher asked them first to plan what they would do and identify what they would need in terms of equipment. Their thinking was probed about what variables to control and what to observe or measure by questions such as: 'How will you be sure that the difference is only caused by the type of soil?', 'How will you be able to show the difference?' Chris had ideas, gathered from various sources, about useful approaches but kept these from the children, only to be introduced if they did not produce ideas of their own. The children were encouraged to make notes of what they found as they went along and then use these notes to prepare a report. Each group reported to the whole class. The teacher told them that they should report what they did and what they found, but also say whether it was what they had expected and to try to explain the differences they found.

Activity 1 *continued*

At the end of the practical work and after a period for bringing their ideas together in their groups, each group in turn presented a report, while other children were given the opportunity to ask questions. Chris refrained from making comments at this stage and asked questions only for clarification. When all the reports had been given, the findings were listed for each soil and the children were asked to decide which might be best for growing some seedlings. The choice was not as obvious as some children had initially thought, so they were very keen to try this next investigation and find out what really would happen.

Attention then turned to the samples of soil that the children had brought from home. In order to compare them with the three soils they had investigated, Chris suggested mixing some of each with enough water to loosen the parts from each other and allow the constituents to separate as they settled to the bottom. The children then used these observations and what they had found about soil to predict which might be 'good growing' soils. These samples were then included in the seedling trials.

Before going on to set up the next investigations, Chris asked the children to reflect on which parts of the work just completed they had enjoyed most, which would they do differently if they could start again and what they now felt they could do better than before.

(Adapted from Harlen, 2002, pp. 2–4)

(a)   Identify the key steps taken by the teacher that helped to ensure that the plans were thorough.

  (i)   How was curriculum continuity addressed?
  (ii) How were individual differences catered for?
  (iii) How was progression built into the aims?

(b)   Describe, for each step, what the teacher did and what children did.

(c)   Using your notes, draft a planning framework on flip chart paper as shown in Figure 12.1 and appoint a spokesperson to describe the framework to the other groups.

Activity 2

Use the planning framework from Activity 1 to prepare a topic on 'keeping fit'. The focus should be on exercise, diet and lifestyle.

For each heading in the 'need to consider' column, identify what the teacher needs to know and how to find out. Exemplify the teacher's planning by anticipating some activities that the children might undertake. Begin by defining the age group of the children.

Summarise your planning using the framework headings, on flip chart paper.

Appoint a spokesperson to describe your planning.

Activity 3

Take one of the other group's plans from Activity 2. Using the planning framework as a guide, analyse and critically evaluate the plans. Ask yourselves the following questions:

- How well is each of the steps in the framework taken into consideration?
- Are aims and objectives clear?
- Are the aims and objectives justified and appropriately matched to the children's age and experience?
- Is there anything you would like to add?
- Is there anything over which you would exercise caution?

Appoint a spokesperson to summarise your evaluation of the planning.

DISCUSSION AND REFLECTION

Activity 1

The *age* and *previous experience* of the children were the first considerations. Chris consulted the school plans and the children's records and accommodated something of the work that went before, in considering continuity of experience.

In extending children's understanding about plant growth, Chris selected an appropriate *context* for the work but a different one (Growing Food) to that previously studied. An additional advantage of the context for this work would be that children were able to make their own contributions from the outset, by bringing samples of soil from their own gardens.

The teacher's *aims* for developing key skills were illustrated by the fact that every stage in the enquiry framework was addressed. The nature of the children's key ideas about growing plants would emerge in the discussions accompanying the design of the investigations. In this way, reinforcement of ideas and appropriate development could be provided.

As the children's questions and ideas became focused on particular investigations, the teacher, in monitoring how each group worked, was able to make appropriate interventions, according to *individual needs and capabilities*.

By anticipating the sorts of investigation that they might undertake, Chris had an idea of the likely need for *resources* and specific pieces of *equipment*.

When the children described their findings and reflected on what had happened, the teacher's questions enabled *outcomes* to be judged and progress to be assessed.

You might have described some of the activities that the children undertook, in greater detail. The likely content, necessary resources and examples of specific outcomes (representing development of ideas and skills) are important to anticipate, in planning. However, for the purpose of this exercise, the analysis of the planning is intended to be 'content-free'.

In conclusion, a framework for planning can be constructed. This is summarised in Figure 12.1.

General aim	Need to consider
Continuity	*Age* of children
	Experience of children
	Context of work
Progression in skills development	Children's levels of performance
	Appropriate *learning objectives*
	Resources and equipment needs
Progress in developing understanding	Children's current ideas
	Appropriate *learning objectives*
Differentiation	How to group children
	Individuals' needs and *capabilities*
Assessment	*Opportunities and Evidence*

Figure 12.1 Planning framework

Activity 2

In finding out about children's previous experience, you will have referred to the school plans and looked through the class records. If the children have been working with you for some time, your own records will be important. If the children are new to the school, it could be more of a challenge to acquire information about their experience and ability. You will know something of any existing liaison procedures with other schools.

You might have decided on a number of possible contexts for work on 'keeping fit'. A focus on healthy eating, or the body, or on exercise all offer potential. However, work on healthy eating and diet does not lend itself to practical investigations and the use of secondary sources would be appropriate, for some children. Similarly, a study of the human body, to consider lungs, muscles, blood, the heart and circulation, for example, holds limited potential for investigating. However, both could lead to investigations relating to exercise, breathing, fitness and pulse rate.

Learning objectives for developing children's understanding would relate to types of food and possibly drugs; muscles and the skeleton; breathing and lungs, blood and circulation; the heart and pulse rate. For developing skills, appropriate objectives would relate to the opportunity to measure the effect of exercise on pulse rate. Children could measure and record their pulse rates and produce graphs and charts.

Some caution will be needed to ensure that the type of exercise undertaken in this work is suitable for all children and that they are not expected to do anything that they cannot normally do. Similarly, children's willingness or ability to engage with secondary sources will vary and you will judge how to group the children for this sort of work.

Outcomes of the work will be different according to a child's contribution to the group so the teacher will need to anticipate using different sorts of evidence to assess each child's achievement.

Activity 3

In reflecting on the planning framework with which you have engaged in this module a number of concerns might have arisen in your mind. For example, how often do you make time to review plans with colleagues? While the focus in these activities has not been on content, perhaps you would have some concern about your own levels of understanding in some areas of science? There has been reference to records of children's progress. How well do you manage your record-keeping?

If you are working alone and it is difficult to find someone with whom to share your plans from Activity 2, you might like to engage in a form of self-evaluation, by considering the following questions:

- When you are teaching science, how well do you plan and manage the teaching? Why?
- To what extent do you 'lead' the work that children undertake?
- How well do you listen to their ideas and suggestions?
- How successful are you in identifying achievable targets, for individual children?
- How successful are they in achieving them?
- How do you know?

Finally, in order to help you to identify the sorts of things that children can do, as their capabilities in science improve, here is a summary of the important features of progression in science.

Children do the following:

- use language that is increasingly precise and technical;
- make links between experiences and understanding in different areas;
- explain as well as describe;
- move from exploration to structured investigations;
- begin to draw on abstractions and models in order to offer explanations;
- produce increasingly sophisticated records and reports.

REFERENCE

Harlen, W. (2000) *The Teaching of Science in Primary Schools*, 3rd edn, London: David Fulton.

FURTHER READING

Progression and continuity

Asoko, H. and Squires, A. (1998) 'Progression and continuity', in R. Sherrington (ed.), *ASE Guide to Primary Science Education*, Cheltenham: Stanley Thornes, pp. 148–55.

Progression and differentiation

Naylor, S. and Keogh, B. (1998) 'Progression and continuity', in A. Cross and G. Peet (eds), *Teaching Science in the Primary School*, Book Two, Plymouth: Northcote House, pp. 34–58.

Progression

Naylor, S. and Keogh, B. (1997) 'Progression in learning in science', in A. Cross and G. Peet (eds), *Teaching Science in the Primary School*, Book One, Plymouth: Northcote House, pp. 51–63.

Differentiation

Naylor, S. and Keogh, B. (1997) 'Differentiation in teaching science', in A. Cross and G. Peet (eds), *Teaching Science in the Primary School*, Book One, Plymouth: Northcote House, pp. 64–75.
Naylor, S. and Keogh, B. (1998) 'Differentiation', in R. Sherrington (ed.), *ASE Guide to Primary Science Education*, Cheltenham: Stanley Thornes, pp. 140–7.
Qualter, A. (1996) *Differentiated Primary Science*, Buckingham: Open University Press.

Self-evaluation

Moyles, Janet R. (1988) *Self-evaluation: A Primary Teacher's Guide*, Windsor: NFER-Nelson.

Module 13 ICT and science (1)

Using ICT to collect data

INTRODUCTION

This module is concerned with planning the science curriculum to include ICT. The focus is on:

- deciding when it is appropriate to use ICT;
- considering how children can collect data by using sensors;
- the need for evaluation of software;
- the use of spreadsheets and branching databases.

When teachers plan a school's science programme, they probably include some aspects of ICT. By its very nature, science sometimes involves collecting large amounts of data which children have to interpret in order to develop and test ideas. The use of ICT makes it possible to collect and process the data so that valuable time can be spent on *thinking* instead of calculating or drawing graphs and charts. The ICT must be seen as an integral part of the science programme and not as an additional activity. Teachers have to make decisions at the planning stage about which applications will be used. They will decide if the ICT makes learning science *easier or more effective*. The use of ICT should be specifically related to the science learning objectives and should not be used primarily for practice in developing IT skills.

Decisions have to be made about the organisation of the learning. Few classrooms have more than two computers, although most schools now have computer suites where there are banks of computers; often using networked software. The teacher needs to be clear about his or her role when using ICT. At times it will be demonstrating a new application, perhaps to the whole class, through the use of an electronic whiteboard. At other times the teacher will allow children to work in pairs or in groups of three on a task which they can complete independently.

At the heart of the teaching he or she will keep in mind the main aims of science: to develop skills and understanding. When using ICT the children must engage cognitively with the activity. It may be that they are searching the Internet or a CD-ROM for information, it may be that they are collecting data through the use of sensors, adding data to a spreadsheet or making a branching key for others to use. Whatever application they are using, they should be encouraged to ask questions, observe carefully, predict and draw conclusions. They should be given the opportunity to evaluate the use of the ICT and, at the later primary stage, decide for themselves what ICT should be used.

In Activity 1 you are asked to consider what ICT could be included in a planned science programme for a class of 8 and 9 year olds. Each person may have different ideas about what should be done and decisions have to be made about whether or not to use ICT. You will also have to select those applications which would be most effective in teaching and learning. It would not be possible to use all the applications which might be suggested in the time available for science in the curriculum. You will no doubt be familiar with the various applications which are used in the primary school. These typically are:

- a simple pictogram program suitable for very young children;
- a simple word processing program for younger children;
- a word processing program for children aged 8 and above;
- a spreadsheet;
- a database;
- a branching database;
- a graphics program;
- a program to support the use of sensors;
- a program which enables children to prepare a multimedia presentation;
- software to support the use of computer control;
- a digital camera;
- a computer microscope;
- a range of CD-ROMs;
- access to the Internet.

Scientific enquiry is at the heart of the science curriculum. We want children to test out ideas and find answers to questions. In order to do this, children often have to plan an investigation and decide what data they are going to collect. This often involves measurement. The use of sensors allows children to make accurate measurements quickly and accurately. The sensors are usually attached to a box, called an interface, which is attached to the computer. The sensors which are most often used in the primary school measure light, sound and temperature. Sometimes the box and the sensors are used away from the computer in order to take measurements out of doors. This is called data-logging.

The results can be displayed in a variety of ways. Young children can see a colourful bar gauge while older children might interrogate a line graph or a set of measurements in a table in order to find out answers to their questions.

Activity 2 asks you to consider how you might introduce the use of sensors to a class of 6 year olds as they try to find out which is the best fabric to choose if you were making curtains to keep out the light. Activities 3 and 4 are focused on the use of branching databases. These are very useful programs to use in science as they help children to focus observations very closely and to look for similarities and differences in materials, objects and living things. To use these effectively children have to learn to frame questions in a very structured way. Activity 3 involves evaluating software and Activity 4 is concerned with identifying suitable items for inclusion in the branching keys (sometimes called decision trees). Issues of progression will also be considered as children move from making a branching key on paper to considering carefully how to classify a large number of similar objects. The branching keys allow the children to see the process of classification in a visual way.

In Activity 5 you will evaluate a sample spreadsheet and set up your own. Spreadsheets are powerful tools as they show children how ICT can process large amounts of data quickly and easily. However, the teacher and the children must think very carefully about the headings which could be used. Children add data into a row of cells and then the spreadsheets allow children to make calculations such as averages, products, mean, mode and median. They can be used to draw a variety of graphs such as scattergraphs, line graphs, pie charts and block graphs. Children can search for patterns by analysing the data and can add data to their spreadsheet over a long period of time. They can also be used by older children to anticipate what might happen if some of the data was changed. When children do this they are modelling.

THE ACTIVITIES

We live in an age where technological advances are made almost daily. Digital cameras, video recorders, the sending of e-mails, Internet shopping, mobile phones and text messages are commonplace to most of our children.

The children we teach in school are very familiar with computers. Many have computers at home and often use these to play games. We would be doing our pupils a disservice if we did not teach them to use ICT (Information and Communication Technology) in their learning of science. However, teachers have to be very clear about the benefits of using ICT. The software and hardware can be *tools* to develop the *learning of science* but we need to evaluate the provision very carefully before we decide to use ICT. The ICT must enable the children to learn more effectively than they would if ICT were not used.

Naturally we would expect the children's IT skills to be developed as they work in science, but when planning for science learning, the objectives for the lessons should be focused on the science skills and concepts.

Activity 1; Identifying opportunities

In order that a school can plan for continuity in the science curriculum teachers must identify, at the initial planning stage, what the possible uses of ICT might be. They must evaluate the opportunities and consider if ICT would enhance learning.

Here is an outline of some of the science work which a school has planned for the 8 and 9 year olds:

Term 1

Building circuits and testing which materials are insulators and conductors. Identifying the features of solids and liquids and classifying certain materials as either liquids or solids.

Term 2

Examining bones and learning how the skeleton supports the body.
Learning how muscles help movement.
Learning about friction as a force.

Term 3

Learning to use and read thermometers. Finding out which materials are good thermal insulators.
Investigating three habitats:

- a small wood which is close to the school;
- the school garden;
- the pathways around the school.

The school has a computer suite where there are ten networked computers with Internet access. The head teacher has a laptop computer and each class has two additional computers. There are also two digital cameras, a scanner and sensors to measure temperature, sound and light. The school has recently purchased a computer control interface but the staff have not yet had time to learn how to use it. A range of CD-ROMs which provide information about science-related topics is also available as are three tape recorders.

The network programs include:

- a simple pictogram program suitable for very young children;
- a simple word processing program for younger children;
- a word processing program for children aged 8 and older;
- a spreadsheet;

- a database;
- a branching database;
- a graphics program;
- a program to support the use of sensors;
- a program which enables children to prepare a multimedia presentation.

Activity 1

Select one of the topics and then do the following:

- consider whether or not the use of ICT would enhance the teaching of science;
- state what you would use;
- think about what the children might learn;
- consider whether the ICT might be used in an investigation, for collecting information or for interpreting information.

Activity 2; Using sensors

Sensors are often used to collect data in science investigations. The most common sensors used in primary schools are those which monitor light, sound and temperature. Usually sensors are attached to a small box which is plugged into the serial or analogue port of the computer; although, in some packages, the sensors are attached directly into the serial ports. Children can measure the effects of placing the temperature probes into hot and cold places and substances. They can test materials to see which is the best thermal insulator and they can use the light sensors to see which materials allow most light to pass through. Sound sensors can help children to find out which materials muffle sound most effectively or which of a series of drums makes the most noise. The sensors can also be used away from the computer and then connected to the computer so that the data can be interrogated at a later date.

The advantages of using sensors are:

- children can see the results on the screen immediately;
- the information can be presented in a variety of ways such as tables and graphs;
- pupils and teachers can decide how often to take measurements and then these are taken automatically.

Consider the following scenario:

Mr Bold wants to introduce sensors to his class of 6 year olds. His work in science is focused on the topic of materials and he has chosen to do much of the scientific enquiry through the context of homes. The children have made collections of materials which are used in building homes and have observed which are flexible, which are waterproof and which are porous. They have considered why certain materials are used for particular purposes and have been involved in sorting and classifying. He wants the children to learn that some materials are transparent, some are translucent and some opaque. He also wants the children to develop some of the skills of scientific enquiry. He has asked the children: 'How could we decide which fabric would be the best to make curtains which would keep out the light?'

The school has a computer suite where there are ten networked computers and an interactive whiteboard but the teacher has access to this room for only 1 hour each week. However, he also has two computers in the classroom and three light sensors which can all be attached to the computers by interfaces.

It is assumed that before you begin Activity 2 you will have used temperature sensors, light sensors and sound sensors and that you are familiar with the associated software.

Activity 2

What would be the teaching sequence which you would plan if you were Mr Bold? You can assume that he is proposing to spend two one and a half hour sessions on the work over a period of two weeks but also that there will be several 15-minute periods during that time, when small groups or pairs of children can work independently. When planning, consider the anticipated learning outcomes at each stage of the teaching sequence, exactly what Mr Bold and the children might be doing during the lessons and what key questions might be asked.

Activity 3; Using branching databases

Children use branching databases when they are observing and classifying materials, objects and plants and animals. These programs are often introduced when the teacher wants children to learn to use and make classification keys. As children have to ask questions which can be answered by a 'Yes' or 'No' answer, they have to think very carefully about how to frame appropriate questions. Usually, when beginning this type of work, children start with about six simple objects such as pieces of fruit or a collection of pictures of animals and make a sorting key on paper before moving on to work on the computer.

Activity 3

For this activity you will need access to a computer and at least two different branching databases. Imagine that you are working with a group of 7 year olds and that this is their first introduction to branching databases. They have in front of them small pictures of the following:

- cat
- horse
- fly
- blackbird
- fish
- snail.

Try to make a branching key using first one of the programs and then the other. Evaluate the software using the following criteria:

- Ease of use.
- Would children be stimulated by the graphics?
- Are children alerted if they make errors of procedure?
- Is it possible to print out the finished key?
- Would other groups of children be able to use the completed key easily?
- Is there the opportunity for children to add items to the completed key?

Activity 4   Progression in using branching databases

As children become proficient in both their observation skills and their ability to make and use keys, teachers will encourage them to make very detailed observations when classifying. For example, when describing and classifying different types of common insects they may observe features such as body shape, number of legs or the position of antennae. They will make very close observations in order to describe the approximate size of the insects and the colours and patterns on the bodies. They will also develop the ability to make subsets within their classification keys and will deal with greater numbers of items.

In which of these areas of study could branching keys be used?

- Materials including solids, liquids and gases
- Earth and Space
- Plant reproduction

Activity 4 *continued*

- How the heart works
- Healthy eating

If so, could you suggest between six and ten items which could be included in the various keys?

If you do not think that children would benefit from using and making a branching key when studying any of the topics, then *do not* select a list of items for that particular area. Be ready to justify your decisions.

Activity 5 Spreadsheets

Spreadsheets are used when calculations have to be made. At first, the teacher will set up the spreadsheet and the formula to be used for the calculation. Children then add the data into a matrix of cells and, after the calculations have been made, they can use the information to find answers to questions which they and their teachers have posed. The programs can be used to graph data in several forms such as bar charts, pie charts and scattergraphs. As children become more proficient in the use of spreadsheets they will decide for themselves what formula to use and how the data should be arranged in the cells. The spreadsheet can be cut and pasted into other programs to present reports.

Figure 13.1 is a section of a spreadsheet which a group of children and their teacher have set up as part of their investigation into how much carbohydrate children have eaten over a period of time. The teacher set up the headings and the columns and the children keyed in their names and the data.

- What questions could the children ask which could be answered by interrogating the data?
- Is this a good example of the use of a spreadsheet? Would you arrange the column headings in a different way?
- If you were working with your class on a topic concerned with healthy eating, what information would you like the children to collect?
- How could the headings be set up so that the children could sort the information and interrogate the data so that they could learn about the importance of a balanced diet?
- Would you want children to collect data about eating over a long period of time?
- Would you want children to collect data from people of different ages?

If you have access to a computer and spreadsheet software, then perhaps you could set up the column headings of your choice and enter some data which you could collect from colleagues. By doing this you will be able to evaluate the software and the opportunities which it presents for learning science.

Activity 5 *continued*

Name of person	Food eaten	Day 1	Day 2	Day 3	Total
Sam	potato	100	50	50	200
	pasta	0	30	0	30
	cereal	0	0	30	30
	bread	150	25	25	200
				total	460
Fred	potato	0	50	50	100
	pasta	50	0	0	50
	cereal	30	0	0	30
	bread	100	50	50	200
				total	380
Harry	potato	50	25	25	100
	pasta	75	0	0	75
	cereal	0	28	28	56
	bread	25	75	25	125
				total	356
Mary	potato	70	75	0	145
	pasta	0	0	40	40
	cereal	30	35	28	93
	bread	50	25	25	100
				total	378
Susan	potato	0	0	0	0
	pasta	40	0	0	40
	cereal	28	60	25	113
	bread	50	25	35	110
				total	263
Elizabeth	potato	60	35	0	95
	pasta	0	0	30	30
	cereal	25	25	25	75
	bread	30	30	30	90
				total	290
	totals	963	643	521	2127

Figure 13.1 Amount of carbohydrate eaten in a three-day period

DISCUSSION AND REFLECTION

Activity 1

You are asked to consider an outline science programme for 8 and 9 year olds and to decide where ICT might help the children to learn science more effectively. It could be that you decided that ICT would not enhance learning in some of the topic areas but that in some cases there would be many opportunities to use computers. However, decisions have to be made about which applications would be most effective because it will not be possible to find the time or the accommodation for all children to use several applications during the time scale allotted to a single topic area.

If you are working with other people, you could select one area for each group and share your ideas. If you are working alone, then select the area where you think that the use of ICT would be most beneficial.

In the first example children would be learning about circuits and testing materials to find out which are insulators and which are conductors. Since this is essentially an exploration which does not generate a large amount of data, you might consider that the use of ICT is not appropriate. You might draw up a table in which the children can type their results, but the learning of science would not be enhanced. Children who find writing difficult could use a concept keyboard similar to Figure 13.2 to record results.

You may have a CD-ROM which simulates the exploration but this would not be a more memorable or exciting option than testing real materials in the circuits. However, you might think that the use of a branching key when children are identifying the features of solids and liquids would focus children's observations more clearly. Another benefit of using a program such as this would be that children would have to refine their ability to think about the questions which could be asked in order to sort the substances.

Enter	Delete		
Wooden ruler 	Metal scissors 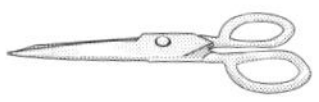	Spoon 	Rubber 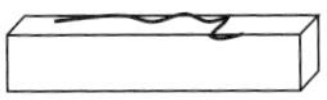
Plastic plate 	Nail 	Does not allow electricity to pass	Allows electricity to pass

Figure 13.2 Example of a concept keyboard overlay

In term 2 the children would be examining bones and learning about how the skeleton supports the body. Although you would want children to look at real bones either by using a human skeleton or animal bones, you will most probably be using secondary sources. There are some useful CD-ROMs which children could use but you might decide that the use of books would provide easier access to the information. Certainly some of the more interactive CD-ROMs are very enjoyable for the children to use. You will have your own views about how to evaluate the support materials. Perhaps you can share ideas with colleagues about suitable resources.

You might have considered that the topic of friction and forces, when children would probably be using force meters, would be a suitable opportunity to use a database or a simple graphing program.

In term 3 the teacher wanted the children to learn how to use a thermometer and to find out which materials are good thermal insulators. There is obviously no substitute for repeated practice if the objective is related to the reading of thermometers, but perhaps a small group of children, who are already proficient at reading thermometers, might use sensors to compare their results with those obtained with the conventional thermometers. You will have probably suggested that when the children are studying habitats there will be opportunities to use databases or spreadsheets and perhaps the use of digital cameras and sensors. However, since all of these would not be used in the same topic you would have to make decisions about which applications to use.

Activity 2

In Activity 2 you are asked to show how a teacher would introduce sensors to a class of 6 year olds as they investigate which fabric would keep out light. This would probably be the first time that the children have used sensors so the teacher could decide to use the electronic whiteboard to demonstrate. It is most important that the children are involved in making decisions about how to test the fabrics and that they see the sensors as tools of measurement. You will also have reflected on how the teacher would help the children to interpret results and to use the terms opaque, transparent and translucent correctly.

Activity 3

Activities 3 and 4 are concerned with the use of branching databases. In Activity 3 you might have shared ideas with colleagues about how this might be done. Children need to learn about the purpose of classification and that we sometimes use keys to help us to do this. You might have used games such as 'Twenty Questions' or the game 'What am I?' where children have to identify an object by asking questions about a small picture which is stuck onto their forehead or a paper hat. The objective of this is to help children to formulate and structure appropriate questions. They may begin by asking 'Is it red?' which would not be as productive as asking 'Am I alive?' When children become more skilful at asking good 'sorting' questions they can move onto making a large key on paper, or with cards and linking strips on which questions are written. The aim of this is for the children to see the pattern of the branching key. Once they can do all this, they are probably ready to use the computer. You will have evaluated the software against the given criteria and may have shared ideas with colleagues.

Activity 4

Activity 4 considers how a branching database might be used by older children. They will use a larger number of items than the younger children and there will probably be sub-sets in the branching key, so for instance if the children were observing invertebrates they might start out by asking 'Does it have legs?' and build up a branch of the decision tree under the 'Yes' answer and another under the 'No' answer.

One of the areas of study is 'How the heart works'. You will have considered whether the making and using of a branching key with items such as aorta, right ventricle, etc. will help children to learn in an enjoyable way. By formulating appropriate questions, children will have to think carefully about the functions of the different parts of the heart.

Activity 5

The emphasis in Activity 5 is on evaluating a section of a sample spreadsheet. Children enjoy both the collection of data and the compilation of spreadsheets, particularly if it concerns themselves. They like to see their own names in the cells. If you were using this type of software with your class, you might decide to suggest questions for the children to answer by interrogating the data or you might ask the children to think of questions which their friends could answer.

Using this example, you will probably have suggested that one of the questions would be about who eats the most carbohydrate on a particular day. Graphs showing the amounts eaten by individuals could be generated but, because of the way in which the spreadsheet is set out, it is not possible to compare total amounts of a particular food eaten each day. Children could analyse the graphs showing an individual's consumption but you might have decided that the making and using of this spreadsheet have little value.

There is no doubt that children will be able to practise interpreting data by using a spreadsheet such as this but you will have to consider carefully whether or not they would be learning any science concepts. You will have reflected on this as you set up your own spreadsheet in order to increase the potential for learning.

FURTHER READING

Cross, A. and Peet, G. (eds) (1997) 'Information Technology as essential in primary science', in *Teaching Science in the Primary School*, Plymouth: Northcote House.

Feasey, R. and Gallear, R. (2001) *Primary Science and Information Communication Technology*, Hatfield: Association for Science Education.

Frost, R. (1996) *IT in Primary Science*, Hatfield: Association for Science Education.

Newton, L. and Rogers, L.T. (2001) *Teaching Science with ICT*, London: Continuum.

Straker, A. and Govier, H. (1996) *Children Using Computers*, Oxford: Nash Pollock Publishing.

Teacher Training Agency (1999) *Using Information and Communications Technology to Meet Teaching Objectives in Science Initial Training*, London: Teacher Training Agency.

Underwood, J. and Underwood, G. (1990) *Computers and Learning*, Oxford: Basil Blackwell, p. 97.

Websites

www.kented.org.uk/ngfl/teaching/qca.htlm
www.rogerfrost.com
www.becta.org.uk

Module 14

ICT and science (2)

Using ICT to interpret data and communicate findings

INTRODUCTION

This module is in two parts. The first part considers how children use data to interpret results and to suggest explanations and the second part is focused on the use of CD-ROMs and the Internet.

When you are carrying out the activities you will be reflecting on the following:

- How data collected from sensors might be analysed so that children are able to hypothesise and how the teacher might scaffold the learning.
- The use of databases and the way in which teachers help children to identify what information should be collected so that the interpretation of data can help them to answer questions which they have raised.
- How simple graphing programs can be used with young children.
- How to evaluate CD-ROMs and websites and how to prepare children so that they search for relevant material which will encourage thinking.

If you have studied Module 13 you will have reflected on the importance of selecting those ICT applications which will make it easier for the children to learn science skills and concepts. In this module we are considering the teacher's role in helping children to make sense of what they find out.

When they are doing science in school, children spend a great deal of time collecting information. For instance, they might weigh and measure each other and record details of eye colour, hair colour and their favourite foods. Often this data is stored either on a spreadsheet or a database. Similar surveys are often done about habitats and environments. We need to ask ourselves how this collection and recording of information can help children to learn science. Is it useful to find out if there are more children who have black hair or brown hair in a particular class? As children scrutinise the graphs and charts, they are learning to interpret information but are they learning science ideas? If, on the other hand, they were linking this information to their parents' hair colour then they might be beginning to learn a little about genetics. What we will be doing in this module is thinking carefully about how the learning can be planned and the importance of providing children with the opportunities to share ideas about what they have found out by looking at the data. The teacher will have particular learning objectives for an area of study and he or she will try to make sure that the information, which is collected and analysed, whether it is from a CD-ROM, a website or from the graphs, which they have generated, will help the children in their learning of science ideas.

In Activity 1 you are asked to read a scenario which describes the work carried out by 8 year olds who were analysing data collected from sensors. You will make comments about the anticipated learning when children are involved in scrutinising the tables and graphs. You may also have some thoughts about the way in which the work was organised. Here you will not only think about the concepts but also about the skills which might be used. You might also consider how the use of the sensors relates to the children's everyday life.

Activity 2 relates to the way in which children can carry out searches when using databases. There is a consideration of the importance of selecting *fields* carefully so that the data provides the opportunity to suggest ideas. So, for instance, as you look at the graph, which shows the height of plants found in a garden, you might consider the potential learning when children scrutinise a graph such as this. Perhaps you might think that a comparison of heights of the same type of plant found in different parts of the garden might be more useful, as it would, perhaps, enable children to compare plants which are in the shade with those growing in full sunshine. The point of this activity is to consider very carefully what children might learn from interpreting information. You are asked to suggest fields which you might set up so that you can maximise the learning opportunities. You are also asked whether you could suggest ways in which children might collect data as a result of investigations as well as, or instead of, carrying out an observational survey.

In Activity 3 you will be suggesting simple investigations which very young children might carry out and which will enable them to display results using a simple graphing program. You will also be considering how a teacher might challenge a child's thinking as he interprets his graphs. There is also the opportunity here to think about other ways of communicating results using ICT. In Module 13 you may have considered this very briefly as part of a planning activity but here you are invited to consider what children might learn by using other forms of ICT.

Activity 4 is focused on the evaluations of CD-ROMs. You are asked to compare two CD-ROMs which have similar content. Teachers will want to make sure that the use of these resources is an integral part of the learning programme and not just an extra activity for those who finish their work before the others.

You are asked to list the key ideas which children might learn by using the resource and to show how you would ensure that children were engaged with the material and were not indulging in pointless browsing. Sometimes children find information about a topic and print out their findings. This in itself will not help the children to learn. You are asked to show how you would guide the children through the learning process and provide them with opportunities to suggest explanations. Children often use CD-ROMs to prepare reports but you will have to make sure that something is done with the report which will facilitate learning. You might think about how the children, who prepared the report, could summarise what they have learned or how they might prepare a list of questions for other children to answer as they read the report. Whatever you decide to suggest, you will keep at the forefront of your mind the cognitive development of the children.

Activity 5 concerns the use of the Internet. You are asked to think about the way in which you would plan for children to access the sites. When children first use the sites you may want to consider providing them with a navigational 'map' in order to guide the search. It will be important for you to review the sites, to which you direct the children, in order to make sure that your learning objectives can be met.

You are asked to prepare a brief critique of a site. The site may be one which is identified in the activities section, or one which you have selected from another source. If you are working with others, there will be an opportunity to share opinions and evaluations. You may want to comment on the ease with which the children can navigate the site, the key ideas which they might learn and the suitability of any simulations which are presented. The main aim of the activity is to consider the children's learning.

Module 13 looks at how teachers make decisions about whether or not to use ICT when children are collecting data. The same decisions have to be made when you are thinking about how children interpret information which they have collected. The interpretation in itself will not necessarily aid cognitive development. It is the way in which children suggest explanations and assimilate new ideas which helps them to make progress in their learning. The teacher has an important role in this process. The use of ICT may help the teacher to plan for this progression in learning, but only if he or she is very clear about how the technology will be useful.

When children are using ICT in science, they have to interpret results and evaluate the scientific evidence. They also have to communicate their findings in a variety of ways. The first part of this module looks at how children interpret findings and communicate their results. The second looks at how the Internet and CD-ROMs are used to gather, interpret and communicate ideas.

Activity 1 Interpreting data collected from sensors

Consider this scenario:

Mr Smith's class of 8 year olds are learning about light. They have done investigations into how shadows are formed and are now learning about how light is reflected. They have explored mirrors and are thinking about how light is reflected off different coloured materials and fabrics. Last week they watched a video about the way in which the lights in a lighthouse are switched on when it becomes dark and this led to a discussion about how sensors are used in everyday life. They discussed the way street lights and intruder warning lights are operated and the part which sensors play in the process. Mr Smith has planned to do an investigation involving children planning a test to find out about the rate at which water warms up if it is placed into plastic bottles which are wrapped in felt samples of different colours and placed near a powerful lamp. He wants the children to understand the distinction between the reflection of light and the absorption of light. He hopes that the investigation will help children to understand why we wear light-coloured clothes when the weather is warm.

He thought that this would be a good opportunity to show the children how light sensors could be used as a tool to collect data and so he arranged his teaching so that he could take one-third of the class at a time into the computer suite to carry out an investigation into the way in which coloured samples of felt reflect light. He had only one computer in the classroom and so he enlisted the help of the head teacher who worked with the rest of the class while he was in the computer suite. The children and the teacher discussed how to carry out the test and decided to hold the sensors 6 cms from different coloured felt samples and to take readings using the sensors. They were very disappointed in the results which showed very little difference between the samples. They thought that perhaps the light from the classroom was interfering with their readings so they decided to try putting the felt around the inside of a beaker and placing the sensor inside. They were pleased to see that this was much more effective.

When all the children in the class had carried out the investigation and had printed out the tables and graphs, they compared their findings. The children realised that this investigation would not have been possible without the use of the sensors, although one child suggested that he brought his father's light meter into school to see if it would do a similar job. Another child pointed out that even if this piece of equipment were used, they would not have been able to draw graphs and tables of results so easily and quickly.

Look at the children's work in Figures 14.2 and 14.3 and consider what the children might have learned by carrying out this investigation. Complete the pro-forma in Figure 14.1 to show (a) what might have been learned and (b) what questions you might ask.

There are a variety of packages available which enable children to carry out similar investigations:

• Ecolog from Data Harvest www.dataharvest.co.uk
• RM Detector with Number Magic from RM www.rm.com

Activity 1 *continued*

- LogIT available from Griffin and George with Junior Insight from Logotron www.logo.com
- RM Investigate software used with LogIT
- First Sense from Philip Harris www.philipharris.co.uk

What might have been learned	What questions might be asked

Figure 14.1 Using sensors: identifying and developing learning

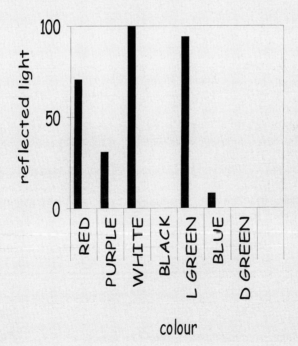

Figure 14.2 Graph produced when investigating reflected light with sensors

Activity 1 *continued*

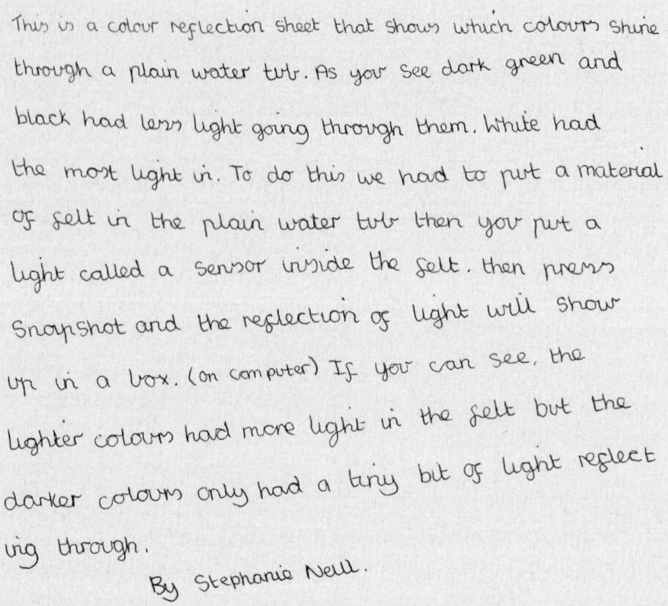

This is a colour reflection sheet that shows which colours shine through a plain water tub. As you see dark green and black had less light going through them. White had the most light in. To do this we had to put a material of felt in the plain water tub then you put a light called a sensor inside the felt. then press Snapshot and the reflection of light will show up in a box. (on computer) If you can see, the lighter colours had more light in the felt but the darker colours only had a tiny bit of light reflecting through.

By Stephanie Neill.

Figure 14.3 Child's account of her investigation with sensors

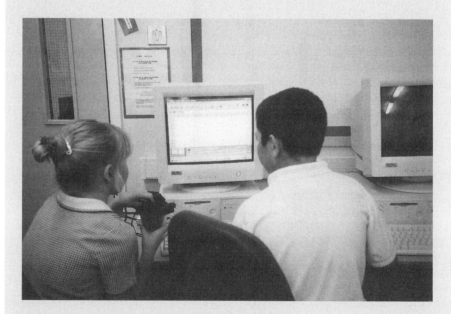

Figure 14.4 Using sensors to find out about reflected light

Activity 2 Searching, sorting and graphing information

Children will need to learn how useful computers can be at searching for information. You can introduce prepared data-files which store information on a wide range of topics such as plants, insects, planets or birds. It is possible to search and sort information very quickly when using these databases whereas using books would take time. Most schools have database software which provides the opportunity for children not only to search ready-made files but also to create their own.

When children are creating a database, they have first of all to decide what sort of information they are going to collect. The information is arranged in categories which are called *fields*. So, for instance, if they were making a database about plants found in the school garden, they might set up fields such as name, colour, where found, leaf shape, flower colour, berries, etc. When the children have filled in all the details about a particular plant they have completed a *record*. There will be a record for each of the plants and when all have been completed, the data can be displayed in a table.

Figure 14.5 is a graph showing the comparative heights of some of the flowers which they might have in the school garden. The teacher will have shown the children how to highlight the area of the table which they want to graph, how to select the type of graph which is most suitable for the purpose and how to label the *x* and *y* axes.

He or she will also have shown the children how to *search* for information so, for example, they could find all plants which were yellow and all plants which are above or below a certain height. They will also learn to *sort* information. In our example they might sort the plants by height or perhaps in alphabetical order. However, perhaps some people might say that there could be more opportunities for learning if children had compared the height of plants of the same type which grow in different places. This would give them the opportunity to consider the effect which light has on plants.

When the teacher is planning to work with databases with the class, he or she has to be mindful of what he or she wants the children to learn. The fields will be chosen with care and after discussion with the children about what they want to find out. Although many databases are compiled as a result of surveys and explorations, sometimes information may be added which is collected as a result of a controlled investigation.

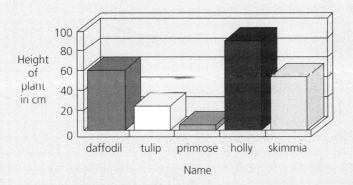

Figure 14.5 Height of plant

Activity 2 *continued*

There are many databases to choose from. If possible, evaluate them before you buy so that you choose those which are most suitable for the various age groups in school. The height of plants graph was produced using *Information Workshop* which operates on different levels for the different age groups. These are suitable for young children:

- First Workshop from RM   www.rm.co.uk
- Information Workshop from RM or Black Cat   www.rm.co.uk
                                                         www.blackcatsoftware.com
- Junior Pinpoint from Longman   www.logo.com
- FlexiDATA from Flexible Software   www.flexible.co.uk

Imagine a group of teachers are planning the use of databases with classes of different ages.

6 year olds	garden plants
7 year olds	invertebrates
8 year olds	ourselves
9 year olds	rocks and soils
10 year olds	air resistance
11 year olds	nutrition

Select two or three of the subject areas and show the following:

- In what particular context the databases could be used.
- What fields could be set up for each of the contexts.
- What questions could children ask as they interrogate the database.
- What specifically the children might learn.
- Whether any of the information could be collected as a result of an investigation.

Activity 3 Communicating results

Sometimes a teacher might want the children to use a simple graphing program to display results of an investigation. This makes the analysis of results easier and the children spend less time on the actual recording. Figure 14.6 shows the work of Charlie and Andrew, 8-year-old boys who had been investigating forces. They used a Newton meter to measure the force needed to pull objects along a table and also to pull open a cupboard. The teacher asked them to draw conclusions and to explain their results. When he went home, Charlie used a spreadsheet on his home computer to draw a similar graph (Figure 14.7).

The simple graphing programs are particularly suitable for use with young children. Some produce pictograms and have the facility for the teacher to use graphics. If we are to encourage the type of scientific enquiry which involves controlling variables then, even at an early age, we can encourage children to interpret simple graphs which they make as a result of their own enquiries.

Activity 3 *continued*

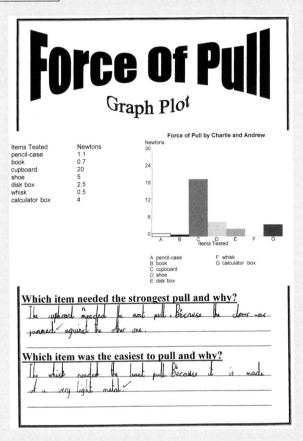

Figure 14.6 Force of pull

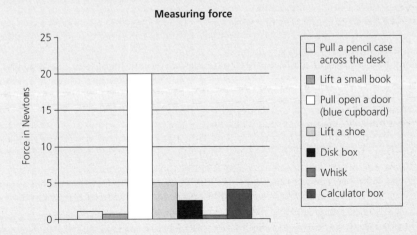

Figure 14.7 Measuring force

Activity 3 *continued*

Here are details of simple graphing programs for younger children:

- Starting Graph from RM   www.rm.co.uk
- Counter from Black Cat   www.blackcatsoftware.com
- Pictogram from Kudlian Software e-mail to   sales@kudlian.demon.co.uk

Now do the following:

(a)   Examine Charlie's work. He is enthusiastic about the use of ICT and enjoys learning. After the investigation, would you have asked him the same questions as those which his teacher asked? Could you suggest other questions which might probe his understanding of forces?

(b)   Imagine that you are working with 5 year olds. Can you think of two simple investigations where results could be displayed easily using a simple graphing program?

(c)   Can you think of other ways of using ICT, apart from graphs, databases and spreadsheets, that might be used to communicate the results of enquiry?

Activity 4   Using CD-ROMs

CD-ROMs are often used as a source of information but they may also encourage children to investigate, predict and suggest explanations. These are the skills which are essential in young scientists. The CD-ROMs present the information in a variety of ways, not only as text but with graphics, video clips and animation. As with all ICT applications, the teacher has to decide whether it will be more beneficial for the children to use the CD-ROM or whether a book would be more useful. The ICT may be amusing and may motivate children but 'aimless browsing through a CD-ROM is as unproductive as aimless browsing through a book' (Straker and Govier, 1996, p. 43). The teacher will review the contents of a CD-ROM before it is used by children and will prepare the children. This might involve asking challenging questions or offering advice about how to access information. Alternatively, the teacher might prepare a writing frame or worksheet which will guide the children through the searching process and identify key questions which need to be answered. The questions might be answered by reading text or looking at a video clip or a picture. When children are recording what they have learned, they may write, draw pictures or diagrams and even produce tables or charts.

If the teacher has access to an electronic whiteboard or a large screen monitor he or she might decide to show parts of the CD-ROM to the whole class after they have carried out their own practical investigations. Many CD-ROMs are interactive and the teacher could ask the children to demonstrate their understanding by completing the 'experiment' section or the 'quiz' section. At all times the teacher will make sure that children are actively engaged with the subject matter and are given opportunities to express their own ideas and offer explanations.

Activity 4 *continued*

www.teem.org.uk, www.becta.org.uk and www.ngfl.org.uk are sites which provide useful information about using CD-ROMs and websites and evaluations of some of the software and websites.

Now do the following:

- Select two CD-ROMs which deal with the same subject.
- Familiarise yourself with the navigational tools and explore the learning opportunities.
- Identify some key ideas which you would want the children to understand after working with the resource.
- Show how you would ensure that children were actively involved with the CD-ROM. If necessary, identify the key questions which you would ask. You might like to sketch out a worksheet which would guide the children through the learning process. Would you use an electronic whiteboard to present the materials to the whole class or would you want children to work in small groups?
- Compare the two CD-ROMs and be prepared to present your findings to your group. If you are working alone then prepare a list of 'pros and cons' related to the two resources.

Activity 5 Using the Internet

If you have 'surfed' the Internet you will know how easy it is to spend hours finding the information which you require. Even when you are quite skilled in selecting appropriate keywords, it is not always easy to find what you are looking for. For this reason perhaps it may be wise to use sites which you have chosen when you first introduce children to the Internet. Anyone can set up an Internet site without any checks being made about the accuracy of the information which is read. The teacher will need to check the site, which he or she intends to use, for accuracy and validity before introducing it to children. There are sites which provide evaluations. One such site can be found at www.teem.org.uk. Some subscription sites have been produced especially for children and most of these are easy to navigate and use simple language. Many allow you to have an introductory period free of charge so that you can evaluate the site. It is wise to do this as even subscription sites do not always provide what you are looking for. A very useful and comprehensive subscription site can be found at www.heinemannexplore.co.uk and another at www.livinglibrary.co.uk. Here are some other useful sites, many of which provide links:

www.techniquest.org
www.exploratorium.edu
www.planet.channel4.com
www.sin.fi.edu/biosci
www.izzy.online.discovery.com

www.yucky.com
www.bbc.co.uk/nature/programmes/tv/blueplanet
www.bbc.co.uk/beasts
www.bbc.co.uk/dinosaurs
www.4learning.co.uk/ict/

Activity 5 continued

www.nasa.gov
www.norcol.ac.uk/nineplanets
www.npac.syr.edu/textbook/kidsweb
www.pfizerfunzone.com/funzone/index
www.brainpop.com
www.4seasons.org.uk
www.tqjunior.thinkquest.org
www.kidshealth.org
www.saps.plantsci.cam.ac.uk
www.virtualfishtank.com/main.html
www.paperairplanes.co.uk

www.channel4.com/science/microsites/
   R/robots
www.yahooligans.com this is a good
   search engine for children
http://kids.msfc.nasa.gov/
www.weboflife.co.uk/weboflife/species-
   web/index.html
www.eskeletons.org/
www.virtualcreatures.com
www.sodaplay.com
www.technosphere.org.uk/

Now choose one of the following:

(a)   www.nhm.ac.uk/education/online/index

Go to the wildlife garden section and click on seasons. You will have the opportunity to answer some questions and to check your answers.

- Would you use this with 10 year olds?
- What would they learn?
- What directions would you give the children as a preparation for using the site?

Explore the rest of the site and prepare a brief critique.

(b)   www.insecta.com

Go to bug of the month and select ladybugs. Prepare a list of questions which you might ask children who were looking at the pictures and reading the text. Would you ask the children to write or draw as they answer your questions?
   Prepare a brief critique of the site and make reference to the reading level of the text and any words which you feel might be unfamiliar to 10 year olds.

(c)   www.askjeeves.co.uk

Ask 'What are ants?' From the selection which appears choose 'ant fact sheet and colouring page'. Prepare a list of questions which you might ask children who were learning about ants. Consider how you would ask the children to respond to your questions. Do you think that this page of the site is suitable to use with 10 year olds? Justify your decision.

DISCUSSION AND REFLECTION

Activity 1

The scenario will have enabled you to discuss the context in which the children collected the data from the sensors. You may have considered how Mr Smith related the work to the use of sensors in everyday life and you may have referred to other examples such as traffic lights or heat sensors which are used to control the temperature in greenhouses.

The children had to solve a problem when they noticed that at the first attempt they did not receive differentiated readings from the sensors. They thought about the reasons why this might have happened and suggested alternative ways of testing. The table and the graph were used to draw conclusions about the way in which some colours reflect more light than others.

The children's report does not show any understanding about why this might be so, but Mr Smith may have thought that this was a very difficult idea for such young children to understand. He went on to discuss with them the reasons why we wear light-coloured clothing when the weather is sunny and here he is asking them to apply their knowledge to a familiar situation. The follow-up investigation with the water, which took place in the classroom, involved children thinking about the absorption of light.

There could be different opinions about whether Mr Smith should have asked children questions about the data initially or whether the questioning should come after the children had extracted the key ideas from the data. Whatever your view on this, you will probably have identified questions which children could answer. These might be related to the identification of those colours which reflect least or most light and could involve children looking for patterns. They could also be extended to the application of the knowledge. For instance, children could be asked to consider why houses in hot countries are painted white or why ice-cream vans are usually light-coloured.

Activity 2

Activity 2 asks you to decide what children might be learning from a study of certain topics and how the selection of the fields should be closely linked to what you want the children to learn. For instance, if you were considering what the children might learn about as they interpreted data, you might have suggested that the 7 year olds who were learning about invertebrates might compile data from a survey of the invertebrates which could be found in the local area and by collecting information from other sources. The analysis of the data could help them to learn about habitats and about the way in which the animals are adapted to their environment. You may have suggested fields such as:

name	number of legs	antennae	number of body parts	where found
colour	size	number of wings	method of movement	predators

Children could be asked to search for all the invertebrates with wings and to suggest why these creatures have wings. They may be asked to find those which have six legs, eight legs, four legs, no legs or more than eight legs. Questions could be asked such as 'Are there any invertebrates with more than six legs which can fly?' Perhaps patterns might begin to emerge and children could be asked questions about camouflage. For instance, if a search is carried out for invertebrates which were found on leaves, then children could be asked if these invertebrates are a similar colour to the leaves on which they were found. There could be questions about those invertebrates which cannot fly and thought can be given as to how they obtain their food. Brightly coloured invertebrates can be identified and the reasons for the colour can be discussed.

What we are helping the children to do is to go beyond the analysis of the data in order to relate what they have found to what they know about the habitat, the predators and the feeding habits of the invertebrates.

Another example focuses on air resistance. There could be a suggestion that this is investigated by children using a wide range of materials which are made into parachutes of different shapes and sizes; some with a hole in the canopy and others without. Fields could be related to the size, shape, hole, length of string, weight on the string and the materials from which they were made. Although the parachutes have to be dropped from a great height in order for the effects to be judged easily, this is, nevertheless, an activity which can generate many ideas if the teacher probes the children's thinking and asks them to predict, giving reasons for their predictions.

Questions which could be asked might be:

- Do the parachutes drop more quickly if there is a hole in the canopy?
- Does the weight on the end of the strings affect the time taken to fall?
- Do the bigger parachutes fall more slowly than the smaller parachutes?
- Does the material from which the parachute is made affect the time taken to fall?

Activity 3

Activity 3 asks you to look at a child's work and to comment on the learning. The teacher has asked him to interpret his graph and to explain the results. He has offered explanations related to what he remembers about the investigation and has applied common-sense ideas to his answer about the cupboard door. He knows that light things need less force to get them moving than heavy things do. Perhaps the teacher might have extended his thinking by asking him if the shape of the object, or the materials from which it was made, could be related in any way to the result. Perhaps, too, he or she could suggest that he goes on to investigate whether the same objects would be more difficult to move if the table was covered with a rough material.

The second part of the activity involves thinking about investigations where the results could be recorded using a simple graphing program. Any simple investigation can be carried out by young children as long as the dependent variable is numeric and the number can be counted and read by the child. Non-standard measures will probably be used. Some examples might be:

- testing balls to observe the height of the bounce;
- testing disposable diapers to see how much water they can hold before they 'drip';
- counting the number of people who could recognise certain smells in smelly pots;
- measuring how far toy cars roll after being pushed down a slope.

The young children who communicate their results in this way will not only be learning some science ideas, but will be able to understand how the interpretation of graphs helps them to draw conclusions; even if they themselves have not been involved in the investigations.

The third part of this activity asks you to consider other forms of ICT which can be used to communicate ideas. You may have suggested the use of word processing software, perhaps linked to a concept keyboard, for the children to write a report. The use of multimedia presentation software could perhaps be used by older children to present their ideas, the results of their investigations and their research.

Activity 4

You will have reflected in Activity 4 on the importance of previewing and evaluating CD-ROMs before you use them with children. You will have had the opportunity to show how the resources, which you have been comparing, provide you with opportunities for children to engage with the material and to show their own thinking. If you have been in a position to share your opinions with others you may have had the opportunity to collate a series of reviews, as you listen and discuss with others.

Activity 5

Activity 5 relates to the use of the Internet. You will have prepared a critique of the site which you have selected and considered how you can encourage children to learn some science ideas and discuss their own ideas.

If you have reviewed the wildlife garden site you may have commented on the reading level of the text. The words would easily be understood by most 10 year olds but the content may be difficult for the children to understand, unless the teacher questions the children closely and adds his or her own explanations. Perhaps you might have suggested that the interactive whiteboard could be used with the whole class so that all the children have the opportunity to listen to the teacher's explanations.

You will have something to say about the simulations. Does the model of the rotating Earth adequately show how the tilt of the Earth has an effect on the intensity of the sun's rays? You could use the site to ask younger children, or children with learning difficulties, to use the photographs in order to answer questions about the changes which they observe at different times of the year. Perhaps you have also suggested that you could ask them to find the temperatures and relate this to the seasonal changes in the plant life.

If you have been reviewing the insecta site and considering how you would help children to interact with the material, you might have made some comment about the limitations of the site. The range of insects which is discussed is limited and the text is not extensive. On the other hand, there is the possibility of using differentiated worksheets to give to children as they explore the site. Those children who have learning difficulties might look at the pictures and answer questions about the colour of the insects, the reasons why ladybirds are red or why they think that some insects have hairs on their legs. Others could answer questions about the feeding habits, how many eggs are laid, when the eggs are laid and about the predators. If you are involved with European children you may have to explain some of the words.

The page of the Ask Jeeves site to which you are referred is from www.zoomwhales.com and is similar to a page from a book. You may decide that children could just as easily use a book, but this has to be balanced against cost and the availability of your resources. Children who access the site in the same way as you have done will find it a very accessible text and you will have been able to produce lists of questions for children to answer which will enable them to learn about ants. You may have some comment about the illustration and about the way in which you might use this.

REFERENCE

Straker, A. and Govier, H. (1997) *Children Using Computers*, Oxford: Nash Pollock Publishing.

FURTHER READING

Cross, A. and Peet, G. (eds) (1997) 'Information Technology as essential in primary science', in *Teaching Science in the Primary School*, Plymouth: Northcote House.
Cunningham, F., Kent, F. and Muir, D. (1997) *Schools in Cyberspace*, London: Hodder and Stoughton.

Feasey, R. and Gallear, A. (2001) *Primary Science and Information Communication Technology*, Hatfield: Association for Science Education.

Frost, R. (1996) *IT in Primary Science*, Hatfield: Association for Science Education.

Newton, L. and Rogers, L.T. (2001) *Teaching Science with ICT*, London: Continuum.

Teacher Training Agency (1999) *Using Information and Communications Technology to Meet Teaching Objectives in Science Initial Training*, London: Teacher Training Agency.

Underwood, J. and Underwood, G. (1990) *Computers and Learning*, Oxford: Basil Blackwell, p. 97.

Module 15   The role of external resources in helping children to learn science

INTRODUCTION

Most of the planned learning and teaching which you do with your pupils will be done inside the school building. However, many teachers want to make links with children's everyday experience and many plan visits into the community. This may be to the seaside, the local supermarket, the brickworks or to a local park. As well as this type of educational visit, teachers plan to take their pupils to field centres where they usually study various habitats. Often these are habitats which cannot be found near the school. The field centres have the added advantage of providing trained countryside rangers or other experts and offer workshops and supplementary materials for both children and teachers.

Many museums offer facilities where children can handle natural objects and sometimes they also provide opportunities for children to carry out scientific enquiry. Interactive science centres are exciting and entertaining places where children can interact with exhibits which are based around a variety of scientific phenomena. These, too, offer support for teachers and workshops for children and often supply teaching packs which include preparatory and follow-up activities for pupils.

This module is concerned with planning work outside the classroom. The activities are related to the use of the school grounds, planning visits into the community and the use of interactive science centres. The legal requirements and health and safety issues are also considered.

Activity 1 discusses health and safety issues. You will be asked to consult the local and national guidelines which provide information about preparing a risk assessment document so that potential hazards can be identified. By identifying the hazards you can consider how the risks might be minimised. For instance, if you were planning to take children to a farm, then you would make sure that children are told not to put their faces against the animals or put their hands in their mouths after feeding the animals. You would be aware of the dangers of eating any animal foodstuffs and of playing near tractors or other farm machinery. If you were planning a visit to the seashore, then you would make sure that all adults and children are aware of the meaning of warning signs and flags and that the dangers associated with tides and cliffs are considered. The ratio of adults to children is discussed and there is some consideration given to the equipment and clothing which may be required.

In Activity 2 you will consider how you might make use of the resources in the immediate vicinity of the school. Much can be done within the school grounds and even schools without gardens and fields can make use of pathways and the school buildings. The environments which you study with the children may be natural or man-made but it will be important to assess the hazards and the learning intentions by making a preliminary visit. You are asked to consider how the work out of doors might be organised so that children have time to reflect on what they have noticed and to raise questions for investigation.

Teachers usually plan at least one educational visit each year which provides the children with the opportunity to relate their learning to the wider community. This work is not necessarily confined to the science curriculum but in Activity 3 you are asked to identify specific science-based learning opportunities both in the field and at school. You are asked to choose one environment from the following:

- a fire station
- a building site
- the seashore

and to think about the learning potential. You are also asked to consider how very small environments such as a puddle or some snow provide unexpected opportunities for learning.

Activities 4 and 5 are related to interactive science centres. There has been a great deal of research into the way in which adults and children learn as they engage with the exhibits. As a result of the research, many of the exhibits are designed to give feedback to the users and then to challenge them further. Sometimes it is possible to engage at different levels depending on the knowledge which the user already has about the specific phenomena which are being investigated. Science centres plan their exhibits on the understanding that not only do the users have great diversity of experience but that they also learn in different ways. They are based on the constructivist view of learning which suggests that we construct our ideas based on what we already know and on our new experiences (see Module 1). The designers try to ensure that there is 'hands-on' but also 'minds-on' (Honeyman, 1995). Instructors are often on hand to help the children to make sense of what they have noticed. These are people who have been trained to question, explain the exhibits and encourage children and adults.

In the past there have been critics of interactive science centres which have been described by their detractors as fun centres which provide 'edutainment'.

There is no doubt that the centres are enjoyable places which families and groups of children can explore together. The teacher has an important role in preparing the children for the visit and in planning follow-up work so that children are able to build on the ideas which they find as they interact with the exhibits. If you watch unsupervised children in the centres you will observe a wide variety of behaviour. Some will appear to be totally absorbed and challenged by the exhibits while some will flit from one exhibit to another, staying only to press every button which they can see. The teacher will make a preliminary visit to the centre before taking pupils and will be able to decide which exhibits are related to the curriculum areas which are being studied by their classes. They will engage with the resources themselves and so will be ready to act as a role model and questioner.

In Activity 4 you are asked to consider the key features of some research and to prepare an observational schedule which could be used at a centre. While in Activity 5 you are asked to look at an image taken at the world-famous Exploratorium in San Francisco and to suggest what questions you might ask and what follow-up work might be done in school.

Further details about interactive science centres can be found at the following websites:

In the United Kingdom

www.catalyst.org.uk
www.eureka.org.uk
www.gsc.org.uk
www.sciencemuseum.org.uk
www.magnatrust.org.uk
www.msim.org.uk
www.sensation.org.uk
www.techniquest.org
www.visitconkers.com

In Australia

www.uow.edu.au
www.questacon.edu.au

In the USA

www.exploratorium.edu
www.sciowa.org
www.csc.clpgh.org
www.sciencecenterct.org
www.sciencedetroit.org
www.slsc.org
www.mdsci.org
www.lhs.berkeley.edu

In Canada

www.osc.on.ca
www.sciencenorth.on.ca

For information world-wide Search for 'Hands-on Science Centers Worldwide' www.cs.cmu.edu/cs

THE ACTIVITIES

As we go through life, we learn something new almost every day. We learn in our homes, when we are out shopping, when we read the newspaper and when we are talking to our friends. If we are put into a situation where we meet a new idea and are given the opportunity to think about the idea, then we are probably going to learn. Education and schooling are not synonymous, indeed, much of children's learning is done out of school.

Although most of the teaching, which is provided by schools, is carried out within the school building, many links are made to the world outside school. Teachers plan to provide experiences which will reinforce the learning which is done in the classroom. The children may visit a park, a woodland area, a beach, a supermarket, a building site or even an outside area within the school grounds. Many teachers also arrange for their children to visit museums or interactive science centres in order for the children to have further opportunities to think about particular science ideas.

This module is concerned with learning outside school. The activities will focus on the health and safety issues which we must think about when we are preparing to take children out of school, the contexts for learning, the planning and the teaching strategies.

Activity 1   Health and safety

Schools have their own regulations about working outside the school boundaries and these are usually based on the local education authorities' guidelines. Governments also provide advice for teachers who are organising educational visits. Read the local guidance in respect of organising school visits.

Imagine that you are planning to take a class of 7 year olds to a local playground in order to look at the way in which the seesaws, swings and other playground equipment are used. The children have been learning about the forces involved in pushing and pulling and in their design technology lessons they have been thinking about how to make stable structures.

- There are twenty-eight children in the class.
- There is a child in the class who is visually impaired.
- The children will walk to the playground which is half a mile from the school. There will be one major road to cross but there is a safe crossing place.

Prepare a 'risk assessment' document for the educational visit and discuss with colleagues the following issues. Prepare a response to the discussion points.

- How many teachers and other adults would accompany the children on the visit?
- Who would be informed of the details of the visit and how would you pass this information to them?
- What would the children carry with them? What would you and the other adults carry?
- Would the children need any special clothing?

Activity 2   Preparing for learning and teaching

Teachers will prepare for educational visits by making a preliminary survey of the area which is to be studied. The purpose of this visit will be to identify any hazards which may be encountered and to assess the learning potential of the site. The nature of the site will, of course, depend on the science which is to be studied. If, for instance, the teacher wanted children to study various habitats, it would be very sensible to start with a relatively small area such as a section of a hedge, an area of land under a single tree, part of the school garden or a section of a pathway. Children are encouraged to focus carefully on the plants and animals which are found in their 'area', the colour and texture of the soil, the amount of sunlight and shade, as well as the sounds and smells which they notice. If children are to have the opportunity to make connections between the features of the habitat, and the living things which are found there, then teachers will need to make sure that the connections can be made. The preliminary survey will provide them with information about the learning opportunities in various parts of the site. If children are allowed to flit from area to area and to dig randomly in a variety of places, then their study time could be less than fruitful.

Take a brief walk in your immediate surroundings and select an area for study. This doesn't have to be an area which contains living things. It could be a short section of a street, a path, or a building.

Consider the following questions and prepare to present a report to your colleagues:

- What might be the focus of a study here?
- How would you organise the work?
- What questions for investigation might be raised by observing this environment?
- What specifically might the children learn by studying this environment? (You will need to identify a particular age group.)
- Would you study this area more than once during the year?

Activity 3   Identifying the potential for science learning

Because any environmental setting, urban or rural, man-made or natural, is so highly complex, it is essential to provide a focus for work that might be done in it. It is easy for pupil interest and enthusiasm to be dissipated if they are looking at a wide variety of features and aspects on one visit. The exploration and the investigation will be superficial if the focus is not tightly defined. The school's scheme of work will set down the learning objectives for a particular area of study but teachers will decide how and if learning outside school is appropriate.

When teachers arrange for their pupils to work outside the classroom, they have a clear idea about how the resource can stimulate learning. This may not necessarily be confined to work in the science curriculum (see Module 11). However, they must be clear about the anticipated learning outcomes in each of the curriculum areas.

Select one of the environments from list A (larger environments) and list B (smaller environments) in Figure 15.1 and outline the science learning which might develop

Activity 3 *continued*

from a study of the two environments. Make brief notes about the activities which would enable children to learn and identify the specific skills and concepts. Consider what activities might be carried out in the field and what preliminary or follow-up work might be done in the classroom.

List A	List B
A fire station With 7-year-old children	A pile of logs in the school garden With 5-year-old children
A building site With 11-year-old children	A puddle With 6-year-old children
The seashore With 9-year-old children	A blanket of snow in the school playground With 4-year-old children

Figure 15.1 Some suggested starting points

Activity 4 Visiting interactive science centres

In recent years many centres have been set up where children can handle exhibits and manipulate them so that effects can be observed. Interaction means more than just touching (Tuckey, 1992). The exhibits in the centres are designed so that children can explore ideas which they may have about various phenomena. 'Science centres are stimulating, they are visually exciting, noisy, active environments' (Rennie and McClafferty, 1996). The best exhibits encourage children to express their own opinions about what they notice and are, at the same time, designed to motivate children's curiosity. Research (Feher, 1990) has shown that there should be a match between the conceptual level of the learner and the activity and that, in order to learn from the exhibits, 'pupils must have a store of "suitable" concepts' (Tuckey, 1992).

The centres are not without their critics. Shortland suggests, 'When education and entertainment are brought together under the same roof, education will be the loser' (1987, p. 213). There is no doubt that unless children are given the opportunity to think about the science ideas which are demonstrated by the exhibits then there will be little learning. If children are left on their own, many will move from one exhibit to another without thinking about the science ideas which they encounter.

The centres are popular with both children and adults but the teacher has an important role to play in preparing the children for the visit, working with the children at the centre and in structuring the follow-up work in school. It has been said that teachers should be able to differentiate between 'hands-on' and interactive exhibits. 'Hands-on' implies that the children touch the exhibit. It may be that they feel something, strike something or assemble something. Interactive exhibits involve the learner in making some sort of response which in turn invites further action. It is

---

Activity 4 *continued*

the feedback from the operator's action which personalises the experience and it is this which should provoke thinking.

Perry (1989) suggests that a successful exhibit at a science centre should involve the following:

Curiosity	the visitor is surprised and intrigued
Confidence	the visitor has a sense of personal competence by experiencing success
Challenge	the visitor perceives that there is something to work towards
Control	the visitor has a sense of self-determination and control
Play	the visitor experiences enjoyment and playfulness
Communication	the visitor engages in meaningful social interaction

Boisvert and Slez (1994) describe the behaviour of visitors to an exhibit by referring to three levels of engagement:

Level 1 (involved time) Stands in front of and/or looks at the exhibit but does not read instructions or try it; watches another person use exhibit but does not take part; uses exhibit but not as it is intended to be used.

Level 2 (positive interaction) Reads label and directions; uses exhibit as intended; helps another person to use the exhibit by reading instructions, demonstrating its use or manipulating part of the exhibit.

Level 3 (instructional time) Asks staff/teacher to explain how to use the exhibit or what the exhibit is about; discusses meaning of the exhibit with staff/teacher; shares own ideas and information about the exhibit with staff/teacher.

Imagine that you are intending to take a class of 11 year olds to a science centre. The children have been learning about sound and you hope that the exhibits at the centre will help them in their understanding.

You are intending to make a preliminary visit to the centre where you will observe groups of children as they play and explore. You will also interact with the exhibits yourself. Use the information provided to draw up an observation schedule which will enable you to make a judgement about the effectiveness of the exhibits.

Activity 5 Helping children to reflect

The teacher cannot be with all of the children during a visit to a science centre. Other adults would be helping to supervise the children and it is for this reason that, during the preliminary visit, the teacher will make notes about how to question children in order to make them think. These notes will be shared with all adults who accompany the children.

In Figure 15.2 you can see an image taken after a group of children had assembled a catenary arch at the Exploratorium in San Francisco. The numbered blocks are laid out

Activity 5 *continued*

Figure 15.2 Catenary arch

Source: Photo by S. Schwartzenberg (c) Exploratorium www.exploratorium.edu

onto a horizontal board over an outline of the arch. The board is then tilted slowly until it is in a vertical position. The arch is then standing upright and the base board is lowered. The arch remains in an upright position. The shape of the arch is the same as a hanging chain. You can see two chains in the picture; one is a thin chain and one is a heavy chain. If the chains and the arch are touched very gently, they will sway.

What questions would you ask children when they have assembled the arch? Write these down so that you are ready to share them with your colleagues. Have you any idea why the arch does not fall? There may be several ideas which you can discuss with your colleagues.

DISCUSSION AND REFLECTION

Activity 1

If you are taking children to a playground the preparation involved will not be as intensive as if you were preparing for a residential field trip, nevertheless you have a legal responsibility to keep the children safe while they are in your care. You are asked to prepare a risk assessment document which outlines the antici-pated hazards and the steps which you will take to minimise the risks. You will probably have identified the dangers of the moving playground equipment and noted the need for children to be informed regularly of these dangers.

There is an issue to do with the ratio of adults to children and the number of teachers who should be present. It is necessary to consult your local guidelines on Health and Safety on school visits but they will probably indicate that there should be:

- one adult for every six pupils aged 6 or 7;
- one adult for every ten to fourteen pupils aged 8 to 11;
- one adult for the child who is visually impaired.

You will need to ascertain the location of the toilets and inform the parents in writing about the visit. In some areas there may need to be written permission from the parents for the child to take part in the visit. The headteacher should be informed about all aspects of the visit and a written copy of the risk assessment document will have to be approved. The school office should have details of the contact telephone numbers of all parents or guardians and the mobile phone number of the leader of the visit. All participating adults should be fully informed about the risks and the learning objectives of the visit, and children should be allocated to adults who should be quite clear about their responsi-bilities. A minimum of two teachers should accompany the children and there should be a person who is qualified in first aid in the party. Children will need to have waterproof clothing and you might want to carry notebooks, clipboards and pencils for the children to use on site. A small first aid package should be carried.

Activity 2

This is concerned with identifying opportunities for teaching and learning in the school grounds or in the immediate vicinity of the school. You will need to locate the most fruitful environments so that children can either carry out an observational survey or some aspect of scientific enquiry. You are asked to choose one environment and to consider what may be learned. So, for instance, if you are looking at a section of the pathway, you would probably make notes about the plants which are growing between the stones on the path, and the evidence of wearing on the materials from which the path is made. Are the plants which are growing through the stones as tall as those of the same kind which are growing in soil nearby? What do you notice about the colour of the path? Is there evidence of more wearing down the centre of the pathway where most people walk? Perhaps later children could investigate which paving materials are most resistant to staining and wearing. If you were studying the walls, you might ask questions about the purpose of the dampproof membrane and suggest that children follow up the work out of doors with an investigation into the most effective materials for preventing rising damp.

The school gardens could be a good starting point for investigations into various habitats and comparisons may be made later by groups of children who have studied different areas of the gardens. Perhaps you will suggest that children carry out observations of the same area at different times of the year so that they can note the effects of the changing seasons.

It is wise to restrict children's investigations to a small area unless there is a very structured focus such as 'Where do we find the most worms?' You are asked to consider how the work would be organised. If you want to take all the children out of doors at the same time then you will have to consider supervision and the area which you will use. You might want children to survey different parts of the school grounds and then present a detailed report including questions which they want to investigate. Alternatively, if you want children to learn particular concepts, for instance in a study of materials, you might want them all to look at a particular part of a wall, then you might arrange for groups to visit the same area at different times in the week.

Activity 3

In this activity you will have been thinking about preparing children for an educational visit into the community. Often, while they are out of school, the work will encompass several curriculum areas and you will need to be very clear about what you want them to learn. For instance in the visit to the fire station you will probably have considered work in the area of forces and materials and may have identified questions for investigation such as:

Why do we smother flames?	Which squeezy bottle produces the highest water jet?	How does a siphon work?
Is it easier to lift a load using more than one pulley?	Which material is best for a firefighter's jacket?	How can we make hydraulic systems?

You will have considered the discussion which could take place during the visit. For instance, about the role of the firefighters in not only putting out fires, but rescuing animals and people from dangerous situations. This will lead on to consideration of the use of pulleys and levers, which could be modelled and investigated in school. You might discuss the water pressure and investigate this with a hosepipe in the playground when you return to school.

Whichever topic you chose to discuss, you will have reflected carefully on exactly what you want the children to learn, how this fits into the school's planned programme of learning and what preparatory activities could be carried out in school.

If you considered the puddle or the snow, you will have thought of the way in which we should capitalise on the unexpected. Many children have very limited experience of snow and it would be a pity if we did not make use of it. You might suggest that a carton of snow is brought into the classroom so that the snowflakes can be observed under magnifiers or microscopes. You will probably want to observe the rate at which it melts and, if you are brave enough, you might suggest that the children put on coats and boots, and then you can take them outside and look at the footprints and animal tracks in the snow!

You might suggest that you draw around the puddle and observe it at regular intervals during the day. You will probably consider how to find out the children's ideas about evaporation and consider further work in the classroom such as watching the rate at which a wet handprint disappears from a paper towel or watching washing as it dries on the washing line.

Activity 4

This asks you to consider some of the research into the use of the science centres. If you can read some of the research yourself, you will find that the exhibits have been designed with the research in mind. You will note that it is important for the children to be given opportunities to consider their own ideas and that children learn best if they approach the exhibits with some basic ideas about the phenomena which they will encounter. The websites give further details about the science centres and museums which offer a hands-on and brains-on approach to learning.

You are asked to prepare an observational schedule to use when you make a preliminary visit to a science centre. This visit is essential, as you will be able to work out for yourself exactly how the exhibits encourage you to think and challenge your ideas. You will also find the visit useful in identifying the main concepts which you would like the children to learn. Preparing the schedule may not be easy. You will have to think about how you can judge the attitudes of the children as they play with the exhibits. You will probably want to include some questions which focus on the social interaction and the dialogue which you observe. How can you judge whether there has been some measure of success? The levels of engagement suggested by Boisvert and Slez (1994) may help you to formulate some ideas about how to judge whether the child has understood the main ideas behind the exhibit.

Activity 5

An activity which shows a picture of children who have obviously had success. The sense of wonder and achievement on their faces is apparent. You will probably have reflected on the questions which you would ask as the children built the arch. The blocks appear to be quite narrow and the children will perhaps predict that the arch will topple over when it is tilted into an upright position. You will perhaps have identified points for discussion which will include the forces involved as the blocks push against each other and the bottom blocks push against the table. You will want to point out the shape of the curve and the corresponding curve (a catenary curve) which is made by the hanging chains. You might want to make some link to bridges of this shape which children might have seen.

REFERENCES

Boisvert, D. and Slez, B. (1994) 'The relationship between visitor characteristics and learning-associated behaviors in a Science Museum Discovery Center', *Science Education*, vol. 78, no. 2, pp. 137–48.

Feher, E. (1990) 'Interactive museum exhibits as tools for learning: exploration with light', *International Journal of Science Education*, vol. 12, no. 10, pp. 35–9.

Honeyman, B.N. (1995) 'Science Centres: building bridges with teachers', Paper presented at the A.S.E. conference, Lancaster, January.

Perry, D.L. (1989) 'The creation and verification of a development model for the design of a museum exhibit' (doctoral dissertation, Indiana University, 1989), quoted in L.J. Rennie and T.P. McClafferty, 'Science Centres and science learning', *Studies in Science Education*, vol. 27, pp. 53–98.

Rennie, L.J. and McClafferty, T.P. (1996) 'Science Centres and science learning', *Studies in Science Education*, vol. 27, pp. 53–98.

Shortland, M. (1987) 'No business like show business', *Nature*, vol. 328, pp. 213–14.

Tuckey, C. (1992) 'Children's informal learning at an interactive science centre', *International Journal of Science Education*, vol. 14, no. 3, pp. 273–8.

FURTHER READING

Brooke, H. and Solomon, J. (1992) 'Play or learning? How can primary pupils benefit from an interactive science centre?', *Education in Science*, January, pp. 16–17.

Brooke, H. and Solomon, J. (1996) 'Hands-on, brains-on: playing and learning in an interactive science centre', *Primary Science Review*, October, pp. 14–17.

Martin, M., Brown, S. and Russell, T. (1991) 'A study of child–adult interaction at a Natural History Science Centre', *Studies in Educational Evaluation*, vol. 17, pp. 355–69.

Module 16 Evaluating classroom practice and providing effective feedback to teachers

INTRODUCTION

Monitoring and evaluation may be summed up as:

- monitoring – what is actually happening, and is what is planned actually happening?
- evaluation – what effect do the initiatives or changes have? What is the impact, particularly on pupils' achievements?

There are many aspects to monitoring and evaluating provision in science. High on the national agenda is the issue of standards. How well does the school compare with schools nationally and with similar schools? (Similar schools in the case of England being those with a similar proportion of pupils entitled to free school meals.) National data is available to schools in the form of the school PANDA (Performance and Assessment) which gives comparisons with schools nationally and with similar schools. The 'Autumn Package' also contains helpful statistics and guidance so that schools can plot value-added information as well as absolute statistics.

Planning and the curriculum need to be monitored and evaluated. In England there are non-statutory schemes of work which schools can use. Even allowing for these there will be adjustments needed at individual school and class level to account for the pupils concerned, where differing prior attainment and other factors may come into play.

An important part of monitoring and evaluating provision is work sampling and talking with pupils. This can give revealing insights into pupils' learning and is a cost-effective way of monitoring and evaluating what is being taught, how it is being taught and the extent to which pupils are learning.

The quality of teaching and learning may be best evaluated at first hand by classroom observation. This of course requires release of the co-ordinator and so is costly, but yields much valuable information.

Activity 1 Work sampling

Work sampling can provide some very useful insights into many aspects of science provision in schools. It is routinely carried out as part of the inspection process in England and many schools are finding it a valuable way of collecting information on learning. A range of work needs to be examined covering all age groups in the school and a sample of different attainment needs to be represented within each year group including those pupils with Special Educational Needs.

Which aspects of provision could be monitored and evaluated in this way? For each aspect try to devise a series of questions you would ask yourself, to ensure your examination of pupils' work provided the evaluative judgements you need. Finally, consider the limitations of work sampling for providing evidence for each aspect of provision.

Activity 2 Lesson observation

This activity is in two parts. The first is to list the key features of effective teaching and learning, highlighting any you feel are particularly relevant to science. These can then be shared with other colleagues as appropriate.

The second part of the activity is to read the summary of the two lesson observations and to plan the feedback you would give to the teachers concerned.

Teacher A

A class of Year 5 children have been studying habitats and this has led to a lesson on food chains. The teacher begins the lesson with questions about what the children's favourite foods are. They then talk about the different types of food and revisit previous work on healthy eating. They move on to consider which foods their pets eat.

The teacher's questions are effective in revisiting previous work. Pupils are eager to answer questions and many express the view that foods they particularly enjoy are not always those most healthy. Most recognise that this is not a problem unless their particular preferences are taken to excess. Higher attaining pupils can recall there are major food groups (carbohydrates, proteins and fats) but need help in remembering the scientific terms. Once prompted, however, they remember these. The majority of children can express, knowledgeably, the sort of foods that would make up a healthy packed lunch and recall work they have done in Design Technology in making packed lunches and pizzas.

In discussing the food their pets eat, many are not aware of what is contained in the various foods – 'we just open the packet and feed them!' More are aware of the food wild animals eat and can explain, for example, that lions and tigers eat meat whereas other animals, for example, rabbits and mice, eat plants. Most recognise that humans eat meat and plants, but few appreciate that some humans choose only to eat plants. When the teacher introduces the terms carnivore, herbivore and omnivore, many of the higher attaining pupils have been introduced to these and are familiar with them.

Activity 2 *continued*

The main activity involves sorting pictures of animals into carnivores, herbivores and omnivores. The teacher has differentiated primarily by recording method. Higher attaining pupils record independently by listing the animals under the three headings and writing a definition of each term. They quickly complete their work. Other groups stick pictures in sets and complete definitions in a cloze procedure exercise. The lower attaining group are very confused by the terms and flounder.

Teacher B

A class of Year 6 pupils are carrying out an investigation on friction and which shoe sole will have the best grip. They discuss different types of surface – rough and smooth and which, from personal experience, they have found to produce greater friction and hence have the better grip. Some pupils are familiar with the term friction. They examine the different shoe soles and discuss what they look like and which they feel will provide most friction. Most pupils predict that the rougher and more ridged the surface, the greater the friction. A variety of methods to test out which shoes are suggested, including pulling the shoes along the floor with a Newton meter and placing the shoes on a slope to see which are least likely to slide as the slope is made steeper.

The teacher has provided a range of Newton meters and a good range of different shoe soles as well as some different types of surface to pull the shoes along. Most pupils choose to pull the shoes using a Newton meter and see which are 'hardest to pull'. One group becomes confused as they try the same shoe on different surfaces and lose sight of their original question. Another group uses too smooth a surface so that little difference is observed between the force needed to pull the various shoes along. The teacher intervenes with some good questions to focus pupils on the difficulties they are having, and how they may overcome these, such as trying a rougher surface or putting a mass in the shoes to simulate weight. Some pupils are able to explain that the greater the force needed to pull the shoe, the greater the friction. Most can draw a conclusion about which shoe sole has the best grip. One shoe sole took a lot less force to move it than was expected but the opportunity was not taken to speculate on why this was so.

Activity 3   Looking at standards

'How well are we doing?' and 'How do we compare with other schools?' are important questions to ask. In order to have a view on this, teachers need to be secure in their judgements about standards and if they are high enough. Summative assessment is required (see Module 6). This can be in the form of teacher assessments for a specific part of the curriculum covered to find out if pupils have made appropriate gains in learning, or tests and teacher assessment which compare pupils' performance with other pupils nationally, typically at specified points in a pupil's education. For the

Activity 3 *continued*

former it is important to know what the pupils knew and understood before teaching occurred, in order to judge whether they have made appropriate progress. For the latter, in order to become secure in judgements, teachers need to examine a range of pupils' work and come to decisions about the particular level that the work represents as defined by the National Curriculum, the Scottish 5–14 Guidelines or other locally used curriculum document (see also Module 7).

In deciding how high standards are in the school, what questions would you wish to ask (a) to decide if appropriate progress had been made in a particular unit of work; and (b) if standards at a specified age were high enough?

Activity 4   Talking with pupils

Discussion with pupils is very helpful in establishing the degree of their knowledge and understanding as well as some other aspects of learning such as their attitude to science and what they need in order to improve.

Imagine you are talking with a group of 7 year olds about the work they have been doing on materials. List the sort of questions you would ask to find out the extent of their understanding. Include questions to find out what they understand about scientific enquiry.

Now extend your list of questions to those you would ask of 11 year olds to determine their understanding of dissolving and the factors likely to affect how much or how quickly a substance dissolves.

DISCUSSION AND REFLECTION

Activity 1

Work sampling

This activity considers the importance of work sampling in monitoring and evaluating science provision in school. Aspects of provision that could be monitored in this way include:

1 General compliance with school policies, e.g. marking and presentation.
2 If whole-school planning/schemes of work are being followed.
3 Standards of attainment (in general and of particular groups of pupils, e.g. girls, boys, able pupils, different ethnic groups).
4 Achievement or progress (in general and of particular groups of pupils, e.g. girls, boys, able pupils, different ethnic groups).

5 Continuity and progression.
6 The balance between experimental and investigative science and knowledge and understanding.
7 Teaching.

It is worth noting that work sampling is more manageable if there is a particular focus. This could be in response to a whole-school issue, for example, the use of formative assessment or the extent to which work is differentiated for pupils with differing prior attainment, or a subject specific issue, for example, the extent to which pupils' investigative skills are being developed. Different foci can be covered on different occasions, so ensuring all aspects are monitored and evaluated.

Possible questions include:

1 General compliance with school policies, e.g. marking and presentation:

    (a) Is work neatly presented?
    (b) Is work completed?
    (c) Are corrections or teachers' questions responded to?
    (d) Is a range of recording methods evident?
    (e) Is the work marked?
    (f) Do teachers make corrections?
    (g) Are comments made which indicate why work is good and what needs to be done to help pupils improve?

2 If whole-school planning/schemes of work are being followed:

    (a) Does the work in different year groups correspond to that indicated in the planning?
    (b) Is the amount of depth appropriate or are some teachers over-/under-estimating what is required, resulting in either possible mismatch of work to pupils, repetition in subsequent years or of work already carried out, or gaps in coverage?

3 Standards of attainment:

    (a) Are standards of attainment by the end of Key Stages appropriate taking into account pupils' prior attainment? (It is worth reminding teachers that the baseline assessments made as pupils enter the school are important, as are factors such as mobility.)
    (b) Are there any differences in attainment of boys and girls?
    (c) Are there differences in attainment of different ethnic groups (where this is an issue for the school)?
    (d) Is the attainment of able pupils sufficiently high?
    (e) Is the attainment of SEN pupils as good as it should be taking into account their prior attainment?

(f) Is the attainment of EAL pupils sufficiently high taking into account their stage of acquisition?

4 Achievement or progress:
Are pupils making the progress they should? Similar questions to those in the previous section can be posed. It may be that given their baseline, SEN pupils are making good progress despite not reaching nationally expected levels. Similarly higher attaining pupils could be achieving beyond the national average but not making as much progress as they are capable of.

(a) Is progress better in some year groups or Key Stages than others?
(b) Consider mobility factors. How does the progress of pupils who have been at the school all their school life compare with pupils who have spent less time at the school?
(c) Is progress in experimental and investigative work comparable with that in knowledge and understanding?

5 Continuity and progression:

(a) Does the content in one year build appropriately on that in previous years?
(b) Are there sufficient opportunities for revisiting and reinforcing?
(c) Is there any evidence of checking children's ideas at the outset of a topic, or of assessing their knowledge and understanding at the end to inform future planning?
(d) Is there evidence of progression in the development of children's investigative skills?

6 The balance between experimental and investigative science and knowledge and understanding:

(a) Are sufficient opportunities evident for pupils to learn investigative skills?
(b) Are sufficient opportunities evident for children to carry out a scientific investigation independently (or for younger children, with an appropriate degree of adult support)?
(c) Are investigations used to develop children's knowledge and understanding?
(d) Do children use their knowledge and understanding during investigative work?
(e) Is there an appropriate balance between different areas of knowledge?

7 Teaching:
While the best way to judge teaching is by observation, a number of indicators of the quality of teaching can be found through work sampling. Questions may include:

(a) Is the work sufficiently differentiated for pupils of differing prior attainment?
(b) Is there evidence of teaching investigative skills in a progressive way?
(c) Is the work marked to enable pupils to understand what they have done well and how they may improve?
(d) Is there variety in the recording methods used?
(e) Is there evidence of a range of teaching and learning styles?
(f) Are pupils with SEN sufficiently supported to enable them to demonstrate attainment?

Activity 2

Observation of teaching and judgements of the quality of teaching and learning are now routine in most schools. This is carried out on a regular basis in England by an independent team of inspectors in national inspections, and by headteachers, senior management teams and subject co-ordinators as part of the routine monitoring and valuation of the quality of teaching and learning in schools, and also as part of performance management procedures. Most schools have a specific form that is used for lesson observation. These are often generic, containing typically sections for standards, teaching, learning and pupils' response. Others can be more detailed or subject-specific, an example being found in Newton and Newton (1998, p. 161). Many schools also have protocols for observation of lessons, often as a result of the introduction of performance management and it is important to recognise and work within these. The DfES publication *Embedding Performance Management 2002: Training Modules* (2002) also has sample lesson observation forms and helpful guidance.

The first part of the activity involves you in reflecting upon what you perceive are essential characteristics of good quality teaching and learning. Many texts can be used to supplement your ideas. The OFSTED *Handbook for Inspecting Primary and Nursery Schools* (2000a) (used in inspection in England) contains guidance on making judgements on the quality of teaching and learning. These include for teaching:

- the ability to plan effectively;
- setting clear objectives;
- a good subject knowledge and the ability to select methods and activities to enable pupils to learn effectively;
- the ability to manage pupils well and insist on high standards of behaviour;
- the ability to assess pupils' work effectively and use homework effectively;
- and to use resources including support staff, ICT and equipment effectively.

These are generic and are important indicators of effective teaching. Effective learning is seen as the extent to which pupils

- acquire new skills, knowledge and understanding;
- are productive and work at a good pace;
- understand what they are doing, show interest, maintain concentration;
- can work independently.

Specific subject guidance is available from OFSTED *Inspecting Subjects 3–11: Guidance for Inspectors and Schools* (2000b). Two further useful publications are *Co-ordinating Science across the Primary School* (Newton and Newton, 1998) and *The Primary Co-ordinator and Ofsted Re-inspection* (Gadsby and Harrison, 1999). The former contains a chapter on monitoring and evaluating science teaching and learning and the latter contains a chapter on monitoring your subject area that covers generic and subject specific issues. In particular, there is a very detailed set of questions that will prove useful in classroom observations of teaching and learning.

The second part of the activity involves looking at a brief report of two lessons following an observation. These are deliberately purely descriptive rather than to any prescribed format. Identify the positive aspects of teaching and learning you would wish to identify and those areas for development. Think about the questions you would wish to pose and raise with the teachers concerned. Depending upon your experience you may wish to read more widely on making observations and giving feedback. Guidance should be available from members of the senior management team and may be outlined in a school policy for performance management. Further written guidance is available from the DfES publication, *Embedding Performance Management 2002: Training Modules.*

Some general points to be considered are:

- This sort of classroom observation is not an inspection and the purpose of the observations should be part and parcel of the school focus for observations, be it on general teaching and learning or very specific aspects of science teaching identified as needing investigation as part of raising standards in science.
- To be helpful, it should be a genuine dialogue between the observer and the observed. It is always important to ask the views of the observed. Often from an observer's point of view, there are many issues requiring clarification, for example, why the course of a lesson was changed, why certain decisions were made.
- It is therefore important to decide the most appropriate questions to ask to help to evaluate the lesson; often these can only be decided during the observation, but generic guidance is available in the DfES training package *Embedding Performance Management 2002*.
- Note the positive points first, since almost invariably these will outnumber any development points unless there is a problem.
- Agree the discussion so that both parties feel an appropriate summary of the observation has been made.

- It may be that in some instances concerns with respect to the teaching have been identified which need to be discussed with a member of the senior management team or the headteacher. It should not be expected that instances of unsatisfactory teaching (which can happen to anyone and be a one-off event) should be left to individual co-ordinators.

Activity 3

Looking at standards

In discussing whether appropriate progress has been made in a particular unit of work, a range of issues arise. It is important to be aware of the need to assess where pupils are at the beginning of a unit of work to check if the progress they make is appropriate. Good planning should address issues of continuity and progression (see Module 12), so that work planned is broadly at a level appropriate for a particular age, and more detailed planning can address issues of differentiation. Records of pupils' prior attainment will be useful; however, pupils retain information to varying degrees dependent upon a range of factors such as length of time since the same area was taught, and degree of understanding at the end of the last block of teaching on that topic. It is good practice therefore to have some strategies for finding out pupils' existing ideas, (see Module 1). Planning should address match of work to pupils, so that there are differentiated learning objectives and learning outcomes for pupils. Clear difference in the attainment of pupils would be expected where there are differences in the level of prior attainment, rather than outcomes that are broadly similar, but it would be hoped that there was good value added for all groups of pupils.

Issues which may cause concern might be: those associated with inclusion such as the attainment and progress of different groups, for example, lower attaining pupils or gifted and talented pupils, girls or boys; attainment and progress in different aspects of science such as investigative work compared with knowledge and understanding; whether attainment is broadly what would be expected in terms of the proportion of pupils attaining a threshold level.

In considering if standards at a specified age are high enough, the importance of baseline is an important consideration, so that value added is a key factor and not just the final pupil outcome. National data is available in England in the 'Autumn Package' and comparisons of school test results with national data and similar schools (based upon the proportion of pupils eligible for free school meals) in the form of an individual school 'PANDA' (Performance and Assessment Data). Trends over time are important. Where statistics are based upon teacher assessment, the importance of accuracy of judgements and moderation needs to be considered. Other factors which need to be taken into account include mobility (now recognised as having a significant impact on pupils' attainment), the size of cohorts and the extent to which importance can be attached to variations from year to year. Many education authorities are providing statistical data to help schools to analyse how well they are doing compared with other schools in their area. It may be worth looking at the anonymous PANDA that Ofsted have produced as well as the school's PANDA.

Activity 4

Talking with pupils

Any discussion of this nature is rather artificial, particularly if the children are not well known by the interviewer. Some general questions are advisable to place pupils at their ease, such as about those activities they enjoyed especially. Young pupils are invariably forthcoming and keen to show how much they have learned. It is often helpful for younger pupils to have some concrete materials to explore and to focus discussion around. A selection of different fabrics or rocks may be useful. Typical questions may include the following.
For 7 year olds:

- What is the same about these materials?
- What is different about these materials?
- What do the materials feel like?
- Can you describe the different materials?
- Which sense are you using to describe them?
- How can you sort the materials?
- What are the materials used for?
- What makes them useful?
- Where do the materials come from?
- Can you change these materials?
- What would you like to find or have you found out about these materials?
- How would you decide which rock was the hardest?
- How would you decide which fabric was the warmest?

For 11 year olds:

- Can you tell me what happens when you add sugar to water?
- Why do you think this is happening?
- How is this different from when you add flour to water?
- Do you think there is a limit to the amount of sugar that dissolves in water?
- Can you keep adding sugar to water and it will always dissolve?
- Will a larger amount of water dissolve a larger amount of sugar?
- Does the temperature of the water make a difference?
- Do you know what soluble/insoluble means?
- How would you plan an investigation to find out how the temperature of the water affects how quickly a substance dissolves?

A number of subsidiary questions are likely to arise, for example:

- Which substances would you want to use to dissolve?
- Why?
- How hot would you want the water to be?
- What do you think will happen to the amount of substance that dissolves as the temperature of the water increases?
- If the temperature is warmer will more dissolve?
- What range of temperatures would you wish to use?
- Why is this a good choice of temperatures?
- What will you measure?
- What will you change?
- What will you keep the same?
- How will you decide what effect the temperature has on how quickly the substance dissolves?
- What sort of table would you have to record your results?
- Would you draw a graph? What sort of graph?
- What shape do you think your graph would look like?

REFERENCES

DfES (2002) *Embedding Performance Management 2002: Training Modules*, London: DfES.

Gadsby, P. and Harrison, M. (1999) *The Primary Co-ordinator and OFSTED Re-inspection'*, London: Falmer Press.

Newton, L.D. and Newton, D.P. (1998) *Coordinating Science Across the Primary School'* London: Falmer Press.

OFSTED (2000a) *Handbook for Inspecting Primary and Nursery Schools*, London: HMSO.

OFSTED (2000b) *Inspecting Subjects 3–11: Guidance for Inspectors and Schools*, revised edn, OFSTED website (www.ofsted.gov.uk).

Index